LUKE

The Good News of
God's Mercy

*Jane — These
are the books
we have been
using for our Bible
Study Sessions. I
Checked the ones
we have done
so far - on
the back!*

A Guided Discovery for Groups and Individuals

Kevin Perrotta

LOYOLAPRESS.

CHICAGO

LoyolaPress.

3441 N. Ashland Avenue
Chicago, Illinois 60657

Nihil Obstat
Reverend Charles R. Meyer
Censor Deputatus
March 21, 1999

Imprimatur
Most Reverend Raymond E. Goedert, M.A., S.T.L., J.C.L.
Vicar General
Archdiocese of Chicago
March 25, 1999

The *Nihil Obstat* and *Imprimatur* are official declarations that a book is free of doctrinal and moral error. No implication is contained therein that those who have granted the *Nihil Obstat* and *Imprimatur* agree with the content, opinions, or statements expressed.

The Scripture quotations contained herein are from the New Revised Standard Version Bible: Catholic Edition, copyright © 1993 and 1989 by the Division of Christian Education of the National Council of the Churches of Christ in the U.S.A. Used by permission. All rights reserved. Subheadings in Scripture quotations have been added by Kevin Perrotta.

Jack Dellorto's reminiscence (p. 33) orginally appeared in *God's Word Today* magazine.

The Greek text of the excerpt from a sermon by Cyril of Alexandria (p. 45) can be found in *Patrologia Graeca* 72, edited by J. Migne. Translation by Kevin Perrotta.

Albert Schweitzer's quotation (p. 57) is from his book *On the Edge of the Primeval Forest* (London: A. C. Black, 1924).

The Greek text of the excerpts from a sermon by John Chrysostom (pp. 88–91) can be found in *Patrologia Graeca* 48, edited by J. Migne. Translation by Kevin Perrotta.

Interior design by Kay Hartmann/Communique Design
Illustration by Charise Mericle Harper

ISBN 0-8294-1370-7

Printed in the United States of America
03 04 05 06 07 Bang 7 6 5 4 3

Contents

How to Use This Guide

You might compare this booklet to a short visit to a national park. The park is so large that you could spend months, even years, getting to know it. But a brief visit, if carefully planned, can be enjoyable and worthwhile. In a few hours you can drive through the park and pull over at a handful of sites. At each stop you can get out of the car, take a short trail through the woods, listen to the wind blowing in the trees, get a feel for the place.

In this booklet we'll drive through the Gospel of Luke, making half a dozen stops along the way. At those points we'll proceed on foot, taking a leisurely walk through the selected passages. The readings have been chosen to give a representative sample of Luke's telling of the good news of Jesus Christ. These passages will bring us to the heart of the Christian message.

After each discussion we'll get back in the car and take the highway to the next stop. "Between Discussions" pages summarize the portions of Luke that we will pass along the way.

This guide provides everything you need to explore the Gospel of Luke in six discussions — or to do a six-part exploration on your own. The introduction on page 6 will prepare you to get the most out of Luke's Gospel. The weekly sections feature key passages from Luke, with explanations that highlight what his words mean for us today. Equally important, each section supplies questions that will launch you into fruitful discussion, helping you both to explore Luke for yourself and to learn from one another. If you're using the booklet by yourself, the questions will spur your personal reflection.

Each discussion is meant to be a *guided discovery.*

Guided. None of us is equipped to read the Bible without help. We read the Bible *for* ourselves, but not *by* ourselves. Scripture was written to be understood and applied in and with the church. So each week "A Guide to the Reading," drawing on the work of both modern biblical scholars and Christian writers of the past, supplies background and explanations. The guide will help you grasp Luke's message. Think of it as a friendly park ranger who points out noteworthy details and explains what you're looking at so you can appreciate things for yourself.

Discovery. The purpose is for *you* to interact with Luke's Gospel — and with Jesus, whom Luke describes. "Questions for Careful Reading" is a tool to help you dig into the Gospel and examine it carefully. "Questions for Application" will help you consider what the Gospel means for your life here and now. Each week concludes with an "Approach to Prayer" section that helps you respond to God's Word. Supplementary "Living Tradition" and "Saints in the Making" sections offer the thoughts and experiences of Christians past and present in order to show you what the Gospel has meant to others — so that you can consider what it might mean for you.

How long are the discussion sessions? We've assumed you will have about an hour and a half when you get together. If you have less time, you'll find that most of the elements can be shortened somewhat.

Is homework necessary? You will get the most out of the discussions if you read the weekly material in advance of each meeting. But if participants are not able to prepare, have someone read the "What's Happened" and "Guide to the Reading" sections aloud to the group at the points where they occur in the weekly material.

What about leadership? If you happen to have a world-class biblical scholar in your group, by all means ask him or her to lead the discussions. But in the absence of any professional Scripture scholars, or even accomplished biblical amateurs, you can still have a first-class Bible discussion. Choose two or three people to be facilitators, and have everyone read "Suggestions for Bible Discussion Groups" before beginning (page 92).

Does everyone need a guide? a Bible? Everyone in the group will need their own copy of this booklet. It contains the sections of Luke that are discussed, so a Bible is not absolutely necessary — but each participant will find it useful to have one. You should have at least one Bible on hand for your discussion.

How do we get started? Before you begin, take a look at the suggestions for Bible discussion groups (page 92) and individuals (page 95).

The Purpose of Luke's Gospel — and How to Connect with It

My daughter Virginia called from college recently and told me she had made an important discovery. "I'm coming to realize I don't know myself very well," she said. The school year had been difficult for her in many ways — the worst of it being her roommate's death in a tragic accident. Virginia is a robust, spirited person, but events shook her. By spring she found herself unexpectedly sunk in sorrow and confusion.

I think Virginia's realization may in the long run be more valuable to her than anything she learned in class this year. She is asking new questions about herself and life and God. I don't know if she is planning to read the Gospel of Luke anytime soon, but she might be especially well prepared for it now, since her insight is closely related to an issue we face as we read the Gospel.

The issue is this: Do I see myself as able to make a success of my life through a determined use of my talents and resources? Or do I recognize within myself sources of failure as well as success? Do I, for example, see my tendency to use my talents egotistically, to focus my attention on my own ambitions rather than on the needs of other people? Am I conscious only of my achievements, or am I also aware of my failures to love? Do I focus my attention solely on what I can do in this world, or do I also reflect on the eventual decline of my abilities and the inevitability of my death? In other words, do I see myself as a creature who, along with wonderful gifts, has flaws and limitations?

It is uncomfortable to recognize my weaknesses, my tendencies to evil, my oncoming death, because I cannot fundamentally change these realities. But the central message of the Gospel of Luke is that God has acted to meet my needs. In biblical language, God has brought me salvation: he has come to heal me in the depths of my being, to rescue me from the evils that assail me — to rescue me even from the final disintegration of death. Yet the realization my daughter has been coming to is crucial for me to have as well if I am to receive this divine action. I will be receptive to it only if I recognize my need for it.

The issue of receptivity runs throughout Luke's Gospel. He shows us that God has made salvation available through Jesus of

Nazareth—through Jesus' birth, life, death, and resurrection. In many ways God's action through Jesus was unexpected, even for the Jewish people of the time. As we will see, the salvation Jesus brings goes far beyond what people were looking for—and makes demands on those who accept it. Not surprisingly, then, we meet people in Luke's Gospel who are astonished by Jesus. We see people struggling to understand what exactly *is* the salvation that he offers—and to decide how to respond.

A crucial determinant of people's responsiveness to Jesus is their awareness—or lack of awareness—of any need for God to intervene in their lives. Some people in the Gospel feel no need for what Jesus offers. They think they know where they stand with God, where they are going in life, and how they are going to get there. They think they know themselves.

Others who meet Jesus are not so sure they have it all together. They recognize that they need something from Jesus, although they do not fully grasp what it is. Consequently they are open to the possibility of God's intervening in their lives through Jesus, however unexpected and challenging that may be.

In the sections of Luke that we will be discussing, we read about religious leaders who are satisfied that they are all right even though they suffer a dangerous deficiency of compassion, a kind of malnutrition of the spirit (Weeks 2 and 3). Jesus says to them sharply, "If you're so healthy, you don't need *my* medical services." If only they had made the discovery about themselves that my daughter has been making, they might have examined God's action through Jesus more open mindedly than they do.

Then there are physically sick people who come—or are brought—to Jesus (Week 2). They know they need *something* and are hopeful that Jesus can provide it. While they may have a lot to learn about the nature of their deepest needs, and about Jesus, at least they come.

Among those we will be reading about, the person most realistic about himself is a man who is executed on a cross next to Jesus (Week 5). He has relinquished all illusions about himself. He knows his crimes and acknowledges his total need for God's mercy. Paradoxically, it is this man alone in the Gospel who reaches out to accept the whole rescue from sin and death that God, in his unlimited mercy, offers human beings in Jesus.

This booklet is entitled *Luke: The Good News of God's Mercy.* Presumably, if you have selected it as a discussion guide, you want to experience God's mercy. All of us, I suppose, take up the reading of Luke with at least some awareness of a "presenting problem," as doctors refer to symptoms as the patient experiences them. We know that something in our life, something in ourselves, needs to be set right, forgiven, healed.

At the outset we might ask ourselves whether we are prepared to hear a diagnosis of our condition that is different — perhaps more serious — than our own. Can we suspend for a while our own ideas about who we are, where our life should be going, and what our needs truly are? Are we willing to admit that perhaps we do not thoroughly know ourselves?

We find it prudent to make this admission with regard to physical ailments. We often know where it hurts but not exactly what is wrong or what the remedy might be. That is why we go to a physician, who may be able to determine the underlying problem and do something about it. What happens when our reading brings us in contact with Jesus, the Physician par excellence?

In Luke's Gospel, we will see that the greatest need of some who meet Jesus is to have their eyes opened to their real need. Their lack of compassion, their lack of willingness to put themselves at the service of other people's needs, is a sickness they have not yet recognized. Indeed, their religious behavior serves to hide the problem from themselves. Do we see anything of this in ourselves?

As with the diagnosis, God's remedy may also be different from our expectations. Certainly Jesus meets us at our point of need. When a person with a skin disease comes to Jesus, Jesus heals his skin disease. When a paralyzed man is brought to Jesus, Jesus restores his ability to walk. Jesus is deeply concerned about our "presenting problems." But our deepest needs will be filled not by getting God to do favors for us but by reorienting ourselves toward serving him and the people around us. God's mercy comes to take hold of us and fit us into *his* plans, which may be different from the plans we have fashioned for ourselves. His idea of how he will heal and set us right exceeds what we would have envisioned. Are we willing to have our expectations exceeded?

In the Gospel of Luke we make contact with a will other than our own. God demonstrates that he is not a passive spectator-god who slid a cosmic videocassette into the VCR billions of years ago and now sits back to watch. God is a person who is pursuing a plan, a person who loves, a person who takes the initiative. It is this resolute, initiative-taking God who addresses Mary and reveals his plan for her in Luke's Gospel. As we begin reading the Gospel of Luke, are we prepared to meet this God?

So far we have been focusing on our angle of approach to Luke's Gospel. The foregoing statements have been like the suggestion of a tour guide about the best position from which to look at a site: "Stand over here to get the best view!" But let us also take a few minutes to focus on Luke's Gospel itself. Assuming we have gotten ourselves into an appropriate position from which to view Luke's Gospel, what do we see?

Luke's Gospel is an account in eight parts. Luke has not marked the sections with subheads or chapter titles; the headings (and even the chapter and verse numbers) have been added by translators and editors to help us find our way through the text. Ancient authors had other ways of indicating where the sections of their writings began and ended. Following clues in the text, scholars discern this order:

1. Prologue (1:1 – 4). Luke supplies a brief note on his purpose and method. We won't discuss the prologue, but it takes just a few seconds to read.

2. Birth (1:5 – 2:52). Luke relates the coming of Jesus in tandem with the coming of John the Baptist, who played an important role in launching Jesus' ministry. By telling the stories of their births in parallel, Luke makes it easy for us to see both similarities and differences between them. A similarity is that the conception of both boys is announced by the angel Gabriel; clearly these two are part of a single divine plan to rescue and restore humanity. A difference is that the angel makes the announcement to John's father but to Jesus' mother — underlining the fact that Jesus does not have a human father. God is Jesus' Father; thus Jesus is God's Son. The text for Week 1 comes from this section.

3. Preparation (3:1 – 4:13). John's summons to repentance sets the scene for Jesus' appearance. Jesus is baptized by John and filled with God's Spirit; then his trust and obedience toward God are tested. In its own way this section also carries the message that Jesus is really God's Son. We won't be discussing anything from this section, but the "Between Discussions" pages will say more about it.

4. Ministry in Galilee (4:14 – 9:50). Jesus walks from village to village, announcing that God's plan for meeting humanity's deepest needs is reaching its fulfillment. His healings demonstrate the truth of his message and indicate the life-giving nature of this plan that God is unfolding. These remarkable works also point to Jesus as the crucial agent of God's action.

Jesus instructs people in how to respond to what God is doing, gathers a group of followers, and makes some enemies. The reading for Week 2 gives a taste of this period of Jesus' life — a time when his words and works are making people wonder, "Who is this man?" The section ends in a double climax. Jesus' followers recognize that Jesus is indeed God's designated agent of salvation, and they see a vision in which God himself declares regarding Jesus, "This is my Son, my chosen. Listen to him!"

5. A long trip (9:50 – 19:27). Once Jesus' followers recognize who he is, he begins a long, meandering journey to Jerusalem. There, he knows, he will enter into glory and authority with God by a route that seems unimaginable to his followers — death on a cross. While heading toward this suffering, Jesus spends his time teaching people about God's mercy and about the response of mercy that God wishes to awaken in their hearts. Weeks 3 and 4 offer samples of this teaching.

The travel setting of Jesus' teaching is significant. By giving his instructions as he walks along the road, Jesus shows that putting his teaching into practice is not merely a matter of following directions; it involves following him personally, as his disciples are literally following him on the road he has chosen.

6. Ministry in Jerusalem (19:28 – 21:38). Jesus enters the city like a king and takes his stand as a teacher in the temple. As he does throughout the Gospel, Luke helps us see that Jesus' actions and teaching demonstrate that Jesus is God's Son, his fully authorized agent of salvation.

7. Death (22:1 – 23:56). Having come to Jerusalem expecting to die, Jesus allows a plot to develop against him, and on the night his enemies have chosen, he deliberately waits for them to come and seize him. He is convinced that his death must happen; it is the way designated by God for him to enter into eternal kingship and thus to bring God's salvation into the world. Before his death, he and his followers eat a meal that is heavy with meaning. As he dies, he brings the purpose of his death into sharp focus in a conversation with a fellow dying man. We will read about these moving and profound episodes in Week 5.

8. Resurrection (23:56 – 24:53). Shortly after Jesus' death, his friends discover that his tomb is empty. Then, from his new position of eternal kingship and glory, Jesus appears to his followers. He helps them understand how he will continue to be among them (Week 6). In a final appearance Jesus guides his followers toward the next stage of God's plan for them — the subject of the second volume of Luke's work, called the Acts of the Apostles.

So much for introduction. After the tour bus has arrived at a historical site, and the guide has suggested a suitable vantage point, and we have heard an explanation of the place's significance, then comes the part we made the journey for: we get to see for ourselves. With care and attention, then, let us begin to read Luke, asking the Holy Spirit to bring Luke's words alive as God's words to us.

SURPRISED BY GOD

Questions to Begin

15 minutes
Use a question or two to get warmed up for the reading.

1 How open are you to a major change in your life?
❏ Right now, I really need stability.
❏ Hmm. Depends on what it is.
❏ I'm ready for a change!

2 How do you deal with the unexpected? What is your usual response to change?

3 How has God enriched your life through surprising interventions?

4 In what areas of your life would you most like to see God intervene?

5 minutes
Have someone in the group read "The Reading" aloud. (If participants have not already read "What's Happened," read that aloud also. Otherwise skip it.)

What's Happened

In the Gospel's first episode (1:5 – 25; all citations in this booklet are to Luke unless otherwise noted), Luke relates an incident involving an elderly priest named Zechariah who worked at the Jewish temple in Jerusalem. God sent an angel to Zechariah to tell him that his wife, Elizabeth, who was also no longer young, would soon bear a child — her first. When this child grows up, he will become known as John the Baptist and will prepare people to follow Jesus.

The Reading: Luke 1:26 – 55

A Very Unexpected Announcement

26 The angel Gabriel was sent by God to a town in Galilee called Nazareth, 27 to a virgin engaged to a man whose name was Joseph, of the house of David. The virgin's name was Mary. 28 And he came to her and said, "Greetings, favored one! The Lord is with you." 29 But she was much perplexed by his words and pondered what sort of greeting this might be.

30 The angel said to her, "Do not be afraid, Mary, for you have found favor with God. 31 And now, you will conceive in your womb and bear a son, and you will name him Jesus. 32 He will be great, and will be called the Son of the Most High, and the Lord God will give to him the throne of his ancestor David. 33 He will reign over the house of Jacob forever, and of his kingdom there will be no end."

34 Mary said to the angel, "How can this be, since I am a virgin?"

35 The angel said to her, "The Holy Spirit will come upon you, and the power of the Most High will overshadow you; therefore the child to be born will be holy; he will be called Son of God. 36 And now, your relative Elizabeth in her old age has also conceived a son; and this is the sixth month for her who was said to be barren. 37 For nothing will be impossible with God."

38 Then Mary said, "Here am I, the servant of the Lord; let it be with me according to your word." Then the angel departed from her.

A Joyful Visit

39 In those days Mary set out and went with haste to a Judean town in the hill country, 40 where she entered the house of Zechariah and greeted Elizabeth. 41 When Elizabeth heard Mary's greeting, the child leaped in her womb. And Elizabeth was filled with the Holy Spirit 42 and exclaimed with a loud cry, "Blessed are you among women, and blessed is the fruit of your womb. 43 And why has this happened to me, that the mother of my Lord comes to me? 44 For as soon as I heard the sound of your greeting, the child in my womb leaped for joy. 45 And blessed is she who believed that there would be a fulfillment of what was spoken to her by the Lord."

Mary Declares God's Greatness

46 And Mary said,
"My soul magnifies the Lord,
    47 and my spirit rejoices in God my Savior,
48 for he has looked with favor on the lowliness of his servant.
    Surely, from now on all generations will call me blessed;
49 for the Mighty One has done great things for me,
    and holy is his name.
50 His mercy is for those who fear him
    from generation to generation.
51 He has shown strength with his arm;
    he has scattered the proud in the thoughts of their hearts.
52 He has brought down the powerful from their thrones,
    and lifted up the lowly;
53 he has filled the hungry with good things,
    and sent the rich away empty.
54 He has helped his servant Israel,
    in remembrance of his mercy,
55 according to the promise he made to our ancestors,
    to Abraham and to his descendants forever."

10 minutes
Choose questions according to your interest and time.

1 What does *afraid* mean in verse 30? What does *fear* mean in verse 50?

2 Locate the points where the Spirit of God is mentioned. What kinds of things does the Spirit do?

3 According to Mary's prayer, who is going to benefit from the coming of God's Son? What kinds of benefits will they experience?

4 List the words that describe God's actions in Mary's prayer. Added together, what picture of God do these actions create?

5 In a sentence or two, how would you sum up the central message of this week's reading?

A Guide to the Reading

If participants have not read this section already, read it aloud. Otherwise go on to "Questions for Application."

Our reading begins in Nazareth — today a sprawling working-class town of some seventy thousand residents, but in Mary's day a mere cluster of stone houses, home to perhaps a couple of hundred people. A young woman is indoors, apparently alone, when suddenly an angel appears and addresses her (verses 26–28). There follows a brief but pivotal conversation. By the time the angel leaves, the most important event in history is under way, launched in a village too obscure to be mentioned in any records of the time, through a seemingly insignificant young woman who was probably still in her early teens.

The angel does not spell out in detail the mission God has assigned to Mary's child. But clearly this Jesus will play a decisive part in God's plan. Through Jesus, God will make a permanent change in his relationship with the human race, for Jesus will reign "forever" (verse 33). In previous ages God acted on behalf of human beings in various, somewhat indirect, ways (see Hebrews 1:1). Now he is sending a "special agent" to deal face-to-face with the ills that afflict human beings. The language of kingship indicates that authority will be conferred on Jesus (verses 32–33). As God's Son, conceived by the Spirit, he will be God's personal representative. Indeed, in Jesus, God is coming in person.

The child is the center of attention, but we cannot help noticing the mother also. The disparity between the magnitude of the divine plan and Mary's humble situation makes her a poignant figure. The door to a new era turns on a delicate hinge!

Yet God does not overwhelm this young woman. Gabriel's words show how highly God respects her. As Origen, the Church's first great biblical scholar, pointed out centuries ago, "favored one" — the greeting in verse 28 — was granted by God to no one in the entire Old Testament. This simple greeting, marking the person most favored by God, was reserved for Mary. On other occasions when an angel announced the birth of a child, the dialogue would end after the heavenly messenger gave a final reassurance (for example, 1:20). In Mary's case alone, the messenger waits for a sign of consent (verse 38).

All this demonstrates that God is not *using* Mary; he is commissioning her for a crucial service: raising his Son. He has chosen her for this responsibility (preserving her from sin from her conception, as the Church believes), and he seeks her cooperation. Mary thinks, questions, and then gives herself freely to God's plan. She acknowledges that she is God's servant — literally, in the Greek, his slave — a person who belongs to him fully.

After Gabriel leaves, Mary goes to visit her older relative Elizabeth, who, the angel has told her, has unexpectedly become pregnant. Elizabeth will be a confidante with whom Mary can share her extraordinary experience.

Elizabeth lived roughly ninety miles south of Nazareth, and the trip would have taken Mary four days or more. When Mary arrives, God inspires Elizabeth to recognize the child that Mary is now carrying (verses 41–43). Notice that Elizabeth congratulates Mary not only for being chosen to bear the savior (verse 42) but also for cooperating with God's plan (verse 45). In response, Mary sings God's praises (verses 46–55).

These events present us, like Mary (verse 29), with much to ponder. She experienced God as a person who had an entirely unexpected plan for her life, who intervened at the moment of his choosing, who valued her immensely. Granted, God's plan for Mary was unique; still, we too are in a relationship with this God of the unexpected. What does this mean for us? To Mary, God revealed his intention to make himself present in the midst of ordinary human circumstances. Do we live with an awareness of God's presence in the mundane and seemingly trivial stretches of our lives?

Elizabeth and Mary rejoice (verses 41–55). Not many of us, perhaps, would say our lives are characterized by joy. We may even cringe a little when a homilist takes us to task for not bearing joyful witness to Christ. Where can we find joy? This reading suggests that the source of joy is experiencing God's loving action toward us. The question we need to ask ourselves, then, is whether we grasp that these events in Luke's Gospel are God's actions *for us.*

Questions for Application

40 minutes
Choose questions according to your interest and time.

1 Was Mary taking a risk in saying yes to God's plan? How much of what lay ahead could she have known? When have you taken a significant risk in order to respond to God's invitation? How did you grow spiritually from the outcome?

2 How would you define humility? In her prayer Mary speaks not only about God but also about herself. Is this, then, a humble prayer? Is Mary a humble person?

3 How have you experienced God's plans for your life to be different from your expectations? What have you learned from this?

4 What does today's reading teach about what God values? about what God wants to accomplish? about how God relates to people? How does this differ from your picture of God when you talk with him in prayer? How might this picture of God help you deal with some difficulty in your life right now?

5 What roles of service (major or minor, formal or informal, long-term or short-term) has God commissioned you for? How could you serve him with greater trust that he is with you? (See verse 28.) Do you need to renew your own "let it be with me according to your word" attitude?

6 What is meant by God's mercy? In what way does Mary experience God's mercy (verse 50)? What does her experience indicate about the mercy that God wishes to show us?

"One set of rules I like is the 'list of listens': We will listen carefully to God, to the text, and to one another as we do each study."

Dan Williams, *Starting (& Ending) a Small Group*

Approach to Prayer

15 minutes
Use this approach — or create your own!

✦ Pray the first two joyful mysteries of the rosary, which focus on the annunciation (Gabriel's announcement to Mary) and the visitation (Mary's visit to Elizabeth).

Then give each person the opportunity to mention to God a blessing they are especially grateful for and an area of life where they feel the need of his help and mercy (verse 54). Keep it brief! If you like, continue with a few minutes of conversational prayer for one another's and other people's needs.

Tie it all together by praying Mary's prayer (verses 46–55).

A Living Tradition

Hail, Mary

This section is a supplement for individual reading.

From our reading in Luke comes one of the Church's most popular prayers.

+ Gabriel's greeting (as it was rendered in an old Latin translation) gives us "Hail, Mary, full of grace! The Lord is with you!" (verse 28).

+ Elizabeth's congratulations to Mary supply the addition "Blessed are you among women, and blessed is the fruit of your womb" (verse 42).

+ In the Middle Ages, Christians linked these words, used them as a prayer, and added the name of the fruit of Mary's womb: "Jesus."

Eventually the practice developed of linking fifty Hail Marys into a *rosarium,* or rose garden, the rose being a symbol of joy, and the prayer being a celebration of Mary's joy.

The reading in Luke also supplies us with a warrant for continuing to greet and congratulate Mary in our prayers. Mary declares, "From now on all generations will call me blessed; for the Mighty One has done great things for me" (verses 48–49). In effect, Mary was saying, "From now on people will remark about me, 'The Lord made her truly happy!'"

When we "hail" Mary and declare her truly happy, we remind ourselves where true happiness lies. Mary's happiness, and ours, lies in the God who revealed himself to her—the God who takes the initiative to intervene in human lives and save us.

With Elizabeth, we congratulate Mary not only for her motherhood but also for her response to God (verse 45). This implies a willingness on our part to imitate her. When we go on to say, "Holy Mary, mother of God, pray for us sinners," we are seeking the grace to be able to respond as she did to the God who makes himself present in our lives through Jesus: "Let it be with me according to your word" (verse 38).

Between Discussions

After a lengthy visit, Mary leaves Elizabeth, and Elizabeth has her baby. Zechariah prays a prophetic thanksgiving over their infant son (Luke 1:57–80).

Six months later, now with Joseph, Mary again travels south to the district where Zechariah and Elizabeth live, this time in compliance with a government census requirement. Mary and Joseph arrive in the town of Bethlehem (today a twenty-minute drive from Jerusalem) in time for Mary to give birth. Over this child a prophetic song is also prayed—but not by Joseph. At Jesus' birth, it is not an earthly father but angels who sing (2:8–14)—reminding us that Jesus' Father is in heaven.

From the years between Jesus' infancy and his public life, Luke relates only a single incident (2:41–52). By now it will come as no surprise that this boyhood episode underlines Jesus' relationship with God. Jesus speaks his first recorded words, and they affirm that he must be busy with his divine Father's business (or in his Father's house—the Greek text can be read either way).

Except for that incident, Luke passes over Jesus' life until age thirty. We know only that Jesus grew up in Nazareth, presumably in a small house built on the dry hillside overlooking the green Jezreel Valley. Joseph was a "carpenter"—the Greek word includes someone who worked with stone as well as wood—and Jesus followed him in that line of work. The two of them must have spent many days together, sweating under the potent Mediterranean sun, building and repairing the houses of Nazareth. On occasion they may have climbed north over the hill and walked to the regional capital, Sepphoris, about four miles away, where more jobs might have been waiting.

Suddenly, in the wilderness along the Jordan River, John the Baptist begins to preach. His preaching attracts large crowds (3:1–18). John announces that Israel's history is approaching its climax. God's people have gone astray in sin and are shortly headed toward a final showdown with God's justice. Only by turning their minds and hearts around can they avoid the sentence God is about to pass on their lives. The Judge is already on the way!

Jesus seems to have taken John's preaching as the signal to bring his time in Nazareth to a close. He sets out southward to the place where John is preaching and is baptized by John (3:21). Afterward as Jesus prays, God speaks to him, affirming his unique relationship with the Father: "You are my Son, the Beloved; with you I am well pleased" (3:22).

A period of prayer, fasting, and testing in the wilderness follow this event (4:1–13). The testing revolves around the question of whether Jesus will continue to act as God's Son, trusting and obeying his Father. Jesus passes the test and returns to Galilee, although not to a settled life in Nazareth.

By accepting John's baptism, Jesus signaled his basic agreement with John's message. Yet Jesus will now give the message a different thrust. John proclaimed that God's kingdom was about to arrive. Jesus will proclaim that it is *arriving.*

In his inaugural homily, Jesus quotes an Old Testament prophecy that foretells the coming of God's kingdom and judgment — but Jesus omits the line about judgment (compare Isaiah 61:2 and Luke 4:19). Like John, Jesus believes that God's judgment is coming. But at present, Jesus declares, God's kingdom is breaking into the world with mercy. To demonstrate the nearness of the divine mercy, Jesus accompanies his preaching with healing.

Like John, Jesus is keenly aware that sin cuts people off from God. But Jesus' approach to the problem is different from John's. John called people to repent so that they would be ready for God's coming kingdom. Jesus brings God's kingdom in order to lead people to repentance. The difference is seen in the way John and Jesus conduct themselves. John remains in the wilderness; those who repent go out to him to be baptized. Jesus comes to the towns and homes of people who have not yet repented, demonstrating God's love for them in order to lead them to repentance.

Just as Mary experienced God's intervention in her life when he blessed her with the gift of bearing and raising his Son, so now the people who live in the small towns of Galilee experience God's initiative through Jesus.

An Argument about Dinner

Questions to Begin

15 minutes
Use a question or two to get warmed up for the reading.

1 At large social events
  ❏ I talk with as many people as possible.
  ❏ I like to have one or two in-depth conversations.
  ❏ I'm interested in meeting new people.
  ❏ I'd rather visit with old friends.
  ❏ I avoid large social events.

2 What ingredients make for the success of celebrations such as birthday parties, showers, and wedding receptions? What detracts from their success? What was the happiest celebration you ever took part in? the unhappiest?

3 In what situations do you feel unaccepted? How do you deal with it?

4 When have you asked God for something but received something quite different in response?

5 minutes
Have someone in the group read "The Reading" aloud. (If participants have not already read "What's Happened," read that aloud also. Otherwise skip it.)

What's Happened

Some thirty years have passed, and Jesus has now begun his public activity.

His major action so far has been a kind of keynote address at Nazareth. In it he declared that the time when God would release the poor, the imprisoned, and the sick had arrived — through him (4:16–21). His fellow villagers seemed delighted that one of their own was going to play such a prominent role in God's plans (4:22). One can picture the chamber of commerce members already envisaging the sign: "Welcome to Nazareth, birthplace of Jesus the Wonder-Worker." But then Jesus made it clear that his mission would not provide any special advantages for his hometown (4:23–27) — a declaration that provoked a riot. Jesus narrowly escaped being lynched (4:28–30).

As the Gospel unfolds, we see that Jesus has not come to bring glory to his hometown, nor to make his disciples rich and powerful, nor to uphold the prerogatives of society's leaders, nor even to preserve his own life. He has come simply to show God's mercy to those who need it.

The Reading: Luke 5:12–32

Bringing a Man Back into the Community

¹² Once, when he was in one of the cities, there was a man covered with leprosy. When he saw Jesus, he bowed with his face to the ground and begged him, "Lord, if you choose, you can make me clean." ¹³ Then Jesus stretched out his hand, touched him, and said, "I do choose. Be made clean." Immediately the leprosy left him. ¹⁴ And he ordered him to tell no one. "Go," he said, "and show yourself to the priest, and, as Moses commanded, make an offering for your cleansing, for a testimony to them."

¹⁵ But now more than ever the word about Jesus spread abroad; many crowds would gather to hear him and to be cured of their diseases. ¹⁶ But he would withdraw to deserted places and pray.

"Pardon Me for Dropping In Like This"

[17] One day, while he was teaching, Pharisees and teachers of the law were sitting near by (they had come from every village of Galilee and Judea and from Jerusalem); and the power of the Lord was with him to heal. [18] Just then some men came, carrying a paralyzed man on a bed. They were trying to bring him in and lay him before Jesus; [19] but finding no way to bring him in because of the crowd, they went up on the roof and let him down with his bed through the tiles into the middle of the crowd in front of Jesus. [20] When he saw their faith, he said, "Friend, your sins are forgiven you." [21] Then the scribes and the Pharisees began to question, "Who is this who is speaking blasphemies? Who can forgive sins but God alone?" [22] When Jesus perceived their questionings, he answered them, "Why do you raise such questions in your hearts? [23] Which is easier, to say, 'Your sins are forgiven you,' or to say, 'Stand up and walk'? [24] But so that you may know that the Son of Man has authority on earth to forgive sins" — he said to the one who was paralyzed — "I say to you, stand up and take your bed and go to your home." [25] Immediately he stood up before them, took what he had been lying on, and went to his home, glorifying God. [26] Amazement seized all of them, and they glorified God and were filled with awe, saying, "We have seen strange things today."

Eating with the Wrong Sort of People

[27] After this he went out and saw a tax collector named Levi, sitting at the tax booth; and he said to him, "Follow me." [28] And he got up, left everything, and followed him. [29] Then Levi gave a great banquet for him in his house; and there was a large crowd of tax collectors and others sitting at the table with them. [30] The Pharisees and their scribes were complaining to his disciples, saying, "Why do you eat and drink with tax collectors and sinners?" [31] Jesus answered, "Those who are well have no need of a physician, but those who are sick; [32] I have come to call not the righteous but sinners to repentance."

10 minutes
Choose questions according to your interest and time.

1 Jesus orders the man not to tell anyone about his healing (verse 14). Does verse 15 imply anything about whether the man followed Jesus' instructions? Why did the man act this way?

2 The religious leaders insist that only God can forgive sins (verse 21). Does Jesus disagree with them? Does verse 24 help to answer the question?

3 Reread verse 23. Isn't it equally easy to *say,* "Your sins are forgiven" and "Stand up and walk"? So what point is Jesus making?

4 After criticizing Jesus (verse 21), are the religious leaders among those who praise God for Jesus' action (verse 26)? Does verse 30 help answer this question?

5 If the religious leaders think it is wrong to have dinner with well-known sinners, why are they at Levi's dinner party (verse 30)? Or are they?

A Guide to the Reading

If participants have not read this section already, read it aloud. Otherwise go on to "Questions for Application."

Leprosy is a terrible disease, and its mention in our first episode rivets our attention on the afflicted man's physical condition (verses 12 – 14). But the man probably was not suffering from what we now call leprosy, or Hansen's disease. Scholars think it likely he had some kind of skin disease — psoriasis, for example.

Under the Jewish law, skin diseases made a person ritually impure. Those afflicted were kept apart from other people. This social aspect of his problem was uppermost in the man's own mind: he asks Jesus to *cleanse* rather than *heal* him — cleanse him, that is, from ritual impurity (verse 12). And notice that Jesus sends him to be checked out not by a doctor but by a priest, since only a priest could readmit him to ordinary society by certifying that the ritual impurity was gone (verse 14).

The incident, then, is about a man who wants to regain his normal place in society — and what Jesus does to fulfill that desire.

The typical Galilean house had a flat roof reached by an exterior stairway. So the paralyzed man's friends in the second episode (verses 17 – 26) did not have to be acrobats to perform the feat in verse 19 — although they needed chutzpah to take their neighbor's roof apart!

St. John Chrysostom, a great teacher of Scripture in the fourth century, pointed out, "It is the habit of sick folk to die from their disorder rather than disclose their personal calamities. This sick man, however, when he saw that the place of assembly was filled and the approaches blocked, did not say to his friends, 'Let's wait till the house is cleared. We shall then be able to approach him privately. Why should you expose my misfortunes in the midst of all the spectators?' No, he submitted to being let down through the roof." He must have believed Jesus could heal him.

But the man receives something different from what he expects (verse 20). In Jesus' view, the man's main problem is not paralysis but a ruptured relationship with God. So Jesus forgives his sins. Only then does he heal the man's body — to demonstrate his divine authorization to grant forgiveness (verse 24) and, we may be sure, to show compassion for the man. Did the paralyzed man realize that his sins were a greater problem than his paralysis?

Was he at first disappointed by what Jesus did for him? He must have had a lot to think about afterward.

Levi (verses 27 – 32) was technically a toll collector — a man who held a franchise to collect taxes for the government on goods transported on the roads. Toll collectors made a handsome profit by imposing much higher tariffs than were required — a practice that did not endear them to their fellow citizens. Nothing suggests that Levi was a cut above his colleagues. At least, he seems to have had a lot of friends in the trade (verse 29).

Men and women who valued justice shunned people like Levi. Jesus was concerned about justice, but he was concerned about Levi too. When he passed Levi on the road, he did not ignore him, as most people would. Jesus "looked at Levi carefully," as the Greek of verse 27 literally says. He spoke with Levi (verse 27; as usual, the Gospel condenses a longer conversation into a few words). Jesus went so far as to invite Levi to become one of his followers. (We can imagine how the other disciples felt about having to share a motel room with a tax collector!)

Levi throws a party in Jesus' honor with all the wrong kind of people, and the religious leaders are astonished. The leaders practice a kind of holiness by dissociation (*Pharisee* means "separated one"). If Jesus is a representative of God, they want to know why he would associate with such scum (verse 30).

Jesus replies that God cannot wait for tax collectors and other exploiters of humanity to come to their senses. Sick people can't heal themselves; they need a doctor. God has sent his Son to be with those who hold God in contempt, in order to draw them back into relationship with him (verses 31 – 32).

Jesus, in other words, does not set repentance as a condition of his friendship. He offers people his friendship, hoping it will lead to repentance.

Thus healing of relationships runs as a thread through Jesus' activities. By touch, word, and friendship, he mends people's relationships with God and with one another.

Questions for Application

40 minutes
Choose questions according to your interest and time.

1 Someone has said that the hardest thing to believe God can change is ourselves. Take a minute to think about the greatest problem you face. Reread 5:12. What might you learn from the man's way of coming to Jesus?

2 Who are the "lepers" in your world? How do you relate to them? How could you improve the way you relate to them?

3 Modern society does not operate with a concept of "ritual impurity." But various conditions and disabilities make it difficult for many people to play a normal, active role in society. Can you identify some of these obstacles? Is there a particular action you could take to help someone overcome such an obstacle?

4 Think about your greatest problem. Is it possible that Jesus would identify something else as your greatest need, as he did with the paralyzed man? If so, what implication might this have for your relationship with him?

5 Jesus' approach in verses 29–32 might seem to conflict with the traditional Catholic concern about avoiding bad companions. Does it? Why or why not?

6 Who are the "tax collectors and sinners" in your world? How do you relate to them? How could you relate to them better?

Some questions should be "done alone and not shared. This can help people isolate certain painful areas without fear that they will have to share it with others."

Christine Dodd, *Making Scripture Work*

Approach to Prayer

15 minutes
Use one of these approaches — or create your own!

✦ Invite anyone who has not
already expressed a personal
need to tell the group briefly
about some need. Then be like
the friends of the paralyzed
man, bringing each other to the
Lord: let each person pray for
the needs of the person to their
right. Close your time together
with an Our Father.

✦ When you discussed how Jesus
treated the man with leprosy
and the tax collectors, various
types of people or particular
individuals probably came to
mind. Pray for them now. Go
around the room, each person
offering a brief prayer for those
they think of — and for help in
relating to these people in a
caring, constructive way. Close
with an Our Father.

Saints in the Making

Paralyzed by Guilt

This section is a supplement for individual reading.

Jack Dellorto of Sarasota, Florida, was "paralyzed" after his twenty-year-old son, James Anthony, died in an auto accident.

Terrible guilt weighed on me. I felt I had failed Jim. I was sure that if I had been a more loving father, he never would have died. I experienced dreams in which Jim seemed to beg me for help. As a psychiatric social worker, I knew my obsessive guilt feelings were irrational, but I could not shake them. And I was too ashamed to discuss them.

One Saturday I attended a diocesan Scripture workshop. After participating in an uninspiring group reading of the Gospel passage about Jesus healing a paralyzed man, we were directed to share some personal crisis with a person near us. My crisis was certainly Jim, but I mentioned something else to my neighbor, a nice woman in her fifties. She then revealed a crisis she had kept to herself: she had found a significant lump in her breast and was awaiting biopsy results. Her mother, sister, and several aunts had died of breast cancer, so she was terrified. (The lump turned out to be benign, as she happily reported a few days later.) Moved by her openness, I told her about Jim. She responded with compassion and understanding.

Our group then reread the Gospel passage. We did not sound more in unison, but for me the passage had acquired a new, personal dimension. Through it, I was healed from the paralysis of my grief. I still mourn Jim, but now I am at peace with his death.

Jack offers this insight about his healing:

God's generous grace directed me to "pick up my mat" of worries, repented sin, guilt, and everything else that paralyzed me — and get on with my life. I believe it also helped me to become more compassionate and empathetic. I now carry a different "mat": one of loving forgiveness, hope, and peace.

Between Discussions

Our second reading has given us a sample of Jesus' ministry in rural Galilee. For some months Jesus remains in Galilee, continuing to heal sick people and teach about the kingdom of God (for example, see 9:11) and inviting others, like Levi, to accompany him as he walks from village to village.

The kingdom that Jesus announces is too great a mystery to be summed up in a single statement. Basically it has to do with God's decisive intervention in human affairs. Jesus brings out different aspects of the kingdom at different moments. In one sense the kingdom is the world to come — a final condition of justice and happiness that God will grant human beings according to his judgment at the end of time (13:28 – 29). In this sense the kingdom is coming soon (9:27), although not necessarily right away (19:11). But the kingdom is also God's merciful care for human beings in the present world, and advance signs of it are already springing up in Jesus' activities (17:20 – 21). Although these workings of the kingdom are small-scale at present, the kingdom is so powerful that it will eventually affect the entire world (13:18 – 21).

Kingdom of God can also be translated "reign of God." God's reign is a matter of God's action. Thus Jesus never asks people to *build* the kingdom. God establishes it by his own power. Rather, Jesus challenges us to *enter* the kingdom that God is bringing (18:24 – 25).

Jesus gives increasingly dramatic evidence that God has appointed him as the principal agent of the kingdom. He calms a storm (8:22 – 25), restores the life of a girl who has died (8:49 – 56), and creates enough bread and fish for more than five thousand people to "stuff" themselves (as the Greek literally says — 9:10 – 17). A question forces itself on the disciples: Who *is* this man? Unlike the readers of the Gospel, the disciples have not been told about Jesus' origins and his designation by an angel as God's Son. They have to work out the answer to the question for themselves.

Jesus calls a time-out from preaching and healing to give his followers an opportunity to reflect on his identity (9:18). Peter, who plays the leading role among the disciples, declares the conclusion they have reached: "You are the Messiah" — God's specially chosen agent of salvation (9:20). Jesus tells the disciples to keep their conclusion to themselves (9:21), possibly because they do not yet understand how he will carry out his role.

With Jesus working wonders and attracting favorable attention, his disciples do not expect him to run into implacable opposition from the religious leaders. The idea of a rejected Messiah was contrary to Jewish expectations. Yet in our second reading (5:21, 30) we have glimpsed the displeasure of the religious leaders in rural Galilee.

Jesus announces a divine action that goes beyond the framework of the relationship that God set up with Israel through Moses. This new action is not against Israel. On the contrary, Jesus directs his ministry to his fellow Jews and selects precisely twelve close disciples in order to signal his intention of restoring Israel as God's people (twelve was the number of the tribes of Israel). Nevertheless, some aspects of the Jewish religion will no longer be as important as before. God's new action will cross the boundaries between Israel and the other nations of the world. The temple in Jerusalem will no longer be the locus of God's presence with his people. Understandably, those who are most committed to the existing arrangements — and who benefit most from them — react against the prospect of playing a lesser role in Jesus' version of the restored Israel. The religious leaders see Jesus as a pretender whose claims to act as God's unique, fully authorized agent — indeed, as his Son — are intolerably arrogant (see 5:20 – 21).

Jesus warns his naive followers that the road ahead will not always be lined with admiring crowds (9:22). But they do not grasp his meaning or see what it means for them.

Without waiting for them to understand, Jesus ends his work in Galilee and sets off toward Jerusalem, where he knows he will meet his destined suffering (9:51). The journey turns out to be a long one (stretching from chapter 9 to chapter 19). Along the way, Jesus pauses to engage in the conversation with local religious leaders that is recounted in our next reading.

A Man Had Two Sons

Questions to Begin

15 minutes
Use a question or two to get warmed up for the reading.

1 Where do you fall in the birth order of children in your family? Can you identify one effect birth order has had on you?

2 What was it like for you to leave home? What was your family's response? Was it a peaceful departure? difficult? some of both?

3 Was there ever a point in life when you realized you had made a big mistake? If so, what did you do then?

4 From your observation, how much truth is there in this maxim about how children turn out: The apple doesn't fall far from the tree?

Opening the Bible

5 minutes
Have someone in the group read "The Reading" aloud. (If participants have not already read "What's Happened," read that aloud also. Otherwise skip it.)

What's Happened

Our third reading seems to take up just where the second one left off: some of the religious leaders and Jesus are still discussing his friendship with well-known sinners. In fact, a great deal has happened in the interim. After teaching, healing, disputing with religious leaders, and gathering disciples, Jesus has concluded his activity in Galilee and is now making his way south to Jerusalem.

The recurrence of the debate over Jesus' dining in the homes of tax collectors and sinners shows that this practice was an important feature of his public life. Earlier Jesus used the analogy of a physician to explain his approach. In this reading, he tells an extended parable.

The Reading: Luke 15:1–3, 11–32

The Griping about Jesus' Social Life Continues

1 Now all the tax collectors and sinners were coming near to listen to him. 2 And the Pharisees and the scribes were grumbling and saying, "This fellow welcomes sinners and eats with them." 3 So he told them this parable: . . .

A Headstrong Young Man

11 "There was a man who had two sons. 12 The younger of them said to his father, 'Father, give me the share of the property that will belong to me.' So he divided his property between them. 13 A few days later the younger son gathered all he had and traveled to a distant country, and there he squandered his property in dissolute living. 14 When he had spent everything, a severe famine took place throughout that country, and he began to be in need. 15 So he went and hired himself out to one of the citizens of that country, who sent him to his fields to feed the pigs. 16 He would gladly have filled himself with the pods that the pigs were eating; and no one gave him anything.

17 But when he came to himself he said, 'How many of my father's hired hands have bread enough and to spare, but here I am

dying of hunger! [18] I will get up and go to my father, and I will say to him, "Father, I have sinned against heaven and before you; [19] I am no longer worthy to be called your son; treat me like one of your hired hands."' [20] So he set off and went to his father. But while he was still far off, his father saw him and was filled with compassion; he ran and put his arms around him and kissed him. [21] Then the son said to him, 'Father, I have sinned against heaven and before you; I am no longer worthy to be called your son.' [22] But the father said to his slaves, 'Quickly, bring out a robe — the best one — and put it on him; put a ring on his finger and sandals on his feet. [23] And get the fatted calf and kill it, and let us eat and celebrate; [24] for this son of mine was dead and is alive again; he was lost and is found!' And they began to celebrate.

Not Everyone Is Pleased

[25] "Now his elder son was in the field; and when he came and approached the house, he heard music and dancing. [26] He called one of the slaves and asked what was going on. [27] He replied, 'Your brother has come, and your father has killed the fatted calf, because he has got him back safe and sound.' [28] Then he became angry and refused to go in. His father came out and began to plead with him. [29] But he answered his father, 'Listen! For all these years I have been working like a slave for you, and I have never disobeyed your command; yet you have never given me even a young goat so that I might celebrate with my friends. [30] But when this son of yours came back, who has devoured your property with prostitutes, you killed the fatted calf for him!' [31] Then the father said to him, 'Son, you are always with me, and all that is mine is yours. [32] But we had to celebrate and rejoice, because this brother of yours was dead and has come to life; he was lost and has been found.'"

10 minutes
Choose questions according to your interest and time.

1 Who is the central character in this story?

2 Is there any significance in the difference in the ways the two brothers address their father (verses 12, 18, 21, 29)? What about the difference in the ways the older son and the father refer to the younger son (verses 30, 32)?

3 Who is the older son angry at?

4 Does the father disagree with the older brother's criticism of the younger brother's behavior (see verses 30, 32)?

5 The older brother accuses the father of being unfair. Is he?

6 Are there similarities between the two brothers?

A Guide to the Reading

*If participants have not read this section already, read it aloud.
Otherwise go on to "Questions for Application."*

As in our last reading, the religious leaders fault Jesus for socializing with people who have abandoned God's ways (see 5:29 – 30; 15:1 – 2). To get a feel for why the religious leaders are so offended, try substituting contemporary categories for "tax collectors and sinners" — perhaps "drug dealers and makers of pornographic films."

In response Jesus tells a story that shows the depth of God's mercy — and challenges those who are not willing to pass it on. In a few words he describes a young man who is selfish and stupid in about equal parts. The younger son treats his father as a means to an end — or an obstacle to his end, since the son is impatient for his inheritance but Dad, inconveniently, remains alive. When the father yields to his demand, our young hero puts as much distance as he can between the old homestead and himself. He spends money freely, apparently without making an appointment with a financial planner. Nevertheless, it is hard not to feel sorry for this boneheaded young man when his money runs out and friends are nowhere to be seen. He is reduced to feeding carob pods to pigs — about as low as a Jewish boy can go.

The young man "came to himself" (verse 17), although we may wonder whether he has gauged the depth of his sin. Is his confession a sign of remorse or an expedient for dealing with hunger (verses 17 – 19)?

Clearly he has not gauged the depth of his father's love. He cannot conceive of his humiliated father receiving him back into the family. But the father has been watching the road for his son's return (see verse 20). The father *runs* to the son — an unseemly thing for a respectable gentleman to do. He does not interrogate his son to determine the genuineness of his repentance. Before the son has finished his little speech, the father has already begun surrounding him with signs of acceptance: a robe, a ring, a reception. The father is more concerned about his son's honor than about his own!

Then there is the other son. He is off working in the fields when his good-for-nothing brother makes his appearance. Probably he would have been happier if his brother had *stayed* "dead" and "lost" (verses 24, 32). Yet his anger seems directed not so much at his brother as at his father. The father has been unfair, he complains, not only by welcoming the younger son home but also by making the older son slave away year after year without reward (verse 29). Yet, is the father really demanding and stingy, as the older son perceives him (see verse 31)? Or, in his own way, has the older son also failed to gauge the depth of his father's love? Despite living under the same roof with his father, is he too "dead" and "lost"?

Standing outside the party, the older son faces a moment of decision. Will he also come to his senses? Jesus leaves the question unanswered. His listeners, the religious leaders, must answer the question with regard to themselves, for they are the real-life dutiful "older brothers." What position will they take toward the mercy that God is showing to his real-life wayward children?

For many of us, the older brother is the natural starting point for our reflections on Jesus' story. My own thoughts are provoked by the older brother's attitude toward his father (verse 29). He articulates something I sometimes feel but am reluctant to admit: God expects a lot and seems not to give much in return. As soon as I put the feeling into words, it obviously makes no sense, yet I feel it. It seems I need to hear the father's words (verse 31) as God's answer to me.

Undoubtedly there are times, perhaps many times, when we identify with the younger brother. Until we completely overcome our tendencies to misuse the gifts God has given us, we will have moments of coming to our senses in the midst of messes we have gotten ourselves into. We will always need to learn anew about God's shameless eagerness to forgive us.

Are we also willing to identify with the father? Henri Nouwen asked himself, "Do I want to be like the father? Do I want to be not just the one who is being forgiven, but also the one who forgives; not just the one who is being welcomed home, but also the one who welcomes home; not just the one who receives compassion, but the one who offers it as well?"

Questions for Application

40 minutes
Choose questions according to your interest and time.

1   How do you see yourself reflected in the younger brother? In what ways do you need to arise and return to your Father's house? What steps should you take?

2   What are your motives for repenting of sin? Are they sometimes, or even always, mixed? Do you think this affects God's forgiveness?

3   Has God ever shown you that you underestimated the depth of his love for you? How might your perception of God's love for you affect how you relate to other people?

4   What issues would the younger son have to face after his return? What issues have you had to face after reconciliation with someone?

5 How would you characterize the older son? What do you see of him in yourself? Where do you face a choice like the one he faced?

6 What experiences have taught you the importance of forgiveness? As you have gotten older, have you felt called to the kind of role that the father plays in the story?

"Learning to pray aloud in a group is the most frightening, liberating, terrifying, wonderful thing you, as a Christian, can learn to do."

Norma Spande, *Your Guide to Successful Home Bible Studies*

Approach to Prayer

15 minutes
Use one of these approaches — or create your own!

✦ Let each person offer a brief update on the status of the need they mentioned last time. Invite each person to pray for the person to their right, either renewing the petition for God's help or thanking him for providing what was needed.

Anyone who wishes may offer a spontaneous prayer in response to the reading.

Concluding prayer: "O God, thank you for not resting until you bring me back to you. Help me be like you, loving even when there is no love in return."

✦ Pray Psalms 51 and 103, which express repentance and confidence in God's mercy. If there are four or more people in your discussion group, divide into two groups, and have the two groups pray alternate verses. Conclude each psalm with a Glory to the Father, and end the whole time with an Our Father.

A Living Tradition

The Purposes of the Parable

This section is a supplement for individual reading.

The following excerpt is from a sermon by St. Cyril, a bishop of Alexandria, Egypt, in the fifth century:

Jesus tells the parable of the prodigal son to show that everyone who constantly serves God and leads a truly good and holy life should eagerly follow God's wishes, receiving those who are called to repentance lovingly rather than reluctantly, welcoming happily even those who have committed serious crimes.

Actually we often face this sort of situation. One person leads a fine, virtuous life, while another is weak and is carried down into every kind of evil. It is not unusual for such a person in old age to turn his attention toward God and ask forgiveness of his sins. He becomes a lover of better things — because, I suppose, he will soon have to relinquish earthly life. He asks for baptism, and he gets rid of the charges that God had against him.

This angers some people. "That guy has not even suffered the legal punishments for his crimes. Yet through baptism he has now been esteemed worthy of radiant and admirable grace, he is enrolled among the children of God, he has been honored with the glory of the saints!"

When people spit out mean-spirited things like this, they are not following the aim of the Father of all. For he is filled with joy when he sees those who had been lost being saved and being brought back to their original dignity and freedom. . . .

On the other hand, perhaps you will say to yourself, "I have defiled myself with so many sins, how could I ever be clean again?" You know that you have offended in every way? You acknowledge your sickness? You remember your falls? Then you are close to being saved! For the confession of sins is the beginning of being cleansed. The almighty Lord is not severe or cruel. In fact, he is kind and inclined to be compassionate, knowing how we are made. Confession and flight from evil are a great thing, for they bring us to him. In just this way the dissolute son returned home and was welcomed.

Between Discussions

Y ou may have noticed that our readings so far have all contained references to eating (1:53; 5:29–30; 15:16, 23).
If you read the rest of Luke's Gospel, you would find that eating, as well as talk about eating, is prominent all the way through.
Numerous incidents in Jesus' ministry occur during meals in homes
(7:36–50; 10:38–42; 14:7–24; 19:1–10). Jesus miraculously provides bread and fish for more than five thousand people (9:10–17).
He describes the kingdom of God as a great banquet (14:15–24).
He makes a meal the setting for his final instructions to his disciples
before he dies (22:14–38). When he rises into new life and resumes
his instructions, the conversation soon ends up at a dinner table
(24:13–35).

We modern readers may not catch the significance of all
this dining. It is useful to slip on first-century glasses and see the
eating in Luke's Gospel a little more as it might have looked to
people at the time.

For one thing, getting enough to eat was a much more
urgent concern in the first century than it is for most of us in
the developed world today. Before modern technology, there was
simply less food to go around, and supplies were less certain.
A large proportion of people lived at the subsistence level; that
is, the possibility of starvation was never far away. Most people
at one time or another really did not know where their next meal
was coming from.

In that hungrier first-century world, Jesus' miraculous provision of food created a sensation. Here, indeed, was someone who
could provide what people desperately needed! Here was someone
with life-giving power! What single action could have illustrated the
divine mercy more dramatically than a huge hillside banquet? No
wonder it forms the climax of Jesus' miracles in Galilee.

First-century people also took eating together more seriously than we do. We are often too hurried to do more than eat on
the run. Since our own meals are generally fairly casual, we tend to
take a casual view of the meals in the Gospel. In the first century,
however, meals had an almost sacred importance. Eating together
expressed a bond between people — or created one. Normally you

ate at home with your family. If you ate out, it was likely to be in the home of a relative, friend, or patron, in a religious meeting place with fellow worshipers, or in the hall of a fraternal association. Taking meals in impersonal settings among strangers — eating out in restaurants — was not part of the culture. If you did not have, and did not want to have, a relationship with someone, you would not eat with them. Thus, for example, Jews generally did not eat with non-Jews.

Consider Jesus' practice of dining with tax collectors and sinners from this point of view. In a meals-are-sacred culture, onlookers clearly saw that Jesus was establishing a personal bond with people who scorned justice and other moral values! What a concrete expression of God's desire to have a relationship of friendship and faithfulness with us, even before we show any desire to have such a relationship with him.

For those who were willing to change their ways, like Levi (5:27 – 28) and Zacchaeus (19:1 – 10), dining with Jesus became an experience of reconciliation with God and with his people. The group gathered around the table with Jesus was not a casual intersection of people but an image of the restored community of God's people. In fact, a meal with Jesus was a foretaste of the banquet in the kingdom of God. To dine at table with the king is to be already, in some sense, in his kingdom.

Well, now we ourselves sit at table with Jesus when we celebrate the Eucharist. If we look at the Eucharist through first-century glasses, what features of the celebration stand out more clearly?

No Servant Can Serve Two Masters

Questions to Begin

15 minutes
Use a question or two to get warmed up for the reading.

1 When it comes to eating out
❑ I like a touch of elegance.
❑ Fast food is fine.
❑ I like to experiment. (Want to try that new Afghan restaurant?)
❑ Give me meat and potatoes, thanks.
❑ Volume counts.

2 When you volunteered your time to help a person or a cause, what was your most rewarding experience? your most frustrating experience?

3 What is your experience with homeless people in your town?

Opening the Bible

5 minutes
Have someone in the group read "The Reading" aloud. (If par-
ticipants have not already read "What's Happened," read that
aloud also. Otherwise skip it.)

What's Happened

In our last reading, Jesus explained why he accepted dinner invita-
tions from people who had turned their backs on God. The parable
of the father with two sons conveyed the depth of God's love for
sinful men and women. As the special agent of God's intervention
in the world, Jesus showed this divine love through his friendships
with people who rejected God. Jesus hoped to give them an
experience of God's love for them.

     The parable concluded with a challenge to us, the readers.
As the story ended, the father in the story was pleading with his
older son to come in to the celebration of his brother's return. This
left us asking ourselves how we will relate to those who have turned
away from God and have harmed other people. Will we be dominated by self-righteousness and resentment toward them? Or will
we join with God and be compassionate representatives of his love?

     Thus the parable of the father with two sons addressed
one obstacle to our receiving God's merciful kingdom: self-righteous
judgmentalism. Now Jesus will focus on another obstacle: preoccu-
pation with our own material advancement.

     In the short portion of Luke between our reading last time
and our reading today, Jesus urges his listeners to use their money
to achieve heavenly, rather than earthly, happiness (16:1 – 8). Then
he tells a story to show what it means to use material resources
for heavenly ends. This story, with a few introductory remarks, is
our reading for today.

The Reading: Luke 16:13 – 15, 19 – 31

The Power of Money

[13] "No slave can serve two masters; for a slave will either hate the
one and love the other, or be devoted to the one and despise the other.
You cannot serve God and wealth."

     [14] The Pharisees, who were lovers of money, heard all this,
and they ridiculed him. [15] So he said to them, "You are those who

justify yourselves in the sight of others; but God knows your hearts; for what is prized by human beings is an abomination in the sight of God. . . .

A Rude Awakening

19 "There was a rich man who was dressed in purple and fine linen and who feasted sumptuously every day. 20 And at his gate lay a poor man named Lazarus, covered with sores, 21 who longed to satisfy his hunger with what fell from the rich man's table; even the dogs would come and lick his sores.

22 "The poor man died and was carried away by the angels to be with Abraham. The rich man also died and was buried. 23 In Hades, where he was being tormented, he looked up and saw Abraham far away with Lazarus by his side. 24 He called out, 'Father Abraham, have mercy on me, and send Lazarus to dip the tip of his finger in water and cool my tongue; for I am in agony in these flames.' 25 But Abraham said, 'Child, remember that during your lifetime you received your good things, and Lazarus in like manner evil things; but now he is comforted here, and you are in agony. 26 Besides all this, between you and us a great chasm has been fixed, so that those who might want to pass from here to you cannot do so, and no one can cross from there to us.'

27 "He said, 'Then, father, I beg you to send him to my father's house — 28 for I have five brothers — that he may warn them, so that they will not also come into this place of torment.' 29 Abraham replied, 'They have Moses and the prophets; they should listen to them.' 30 He said, 'No, father Abraham; but if someone goes to them from the dead, they will repent.' 31 He said to him, 'If they do not listen to Moses and the prophets, neither will they be convinced even if someone rises from the dead.'"

Questions for Careful Reading

10 minutes
Choose questions according to your interest and time.

1 In verses 24 and 27 the rich man treats Lazarus as someone who might be sent to run errands—as a social inferior. Why is the rich man still relating to Lazarus this way?

2 Would the story work if the rich man had not known Lazarus during their earthly life? Do any details indicate that he did know Lazarus?

3 Relate verse 15 to the story: What did the rich man prize? Was it "an abomination in the sight of God"? Why?

4 How would you briefly sum up the message—or messages—of the story?

A Guide to the Reading

If participants have not read this section already, read it aloud. Otherwise go on to "Questions for Application."

If the story of the father with two sons is one of Jesus' most consoling parables, the story of the rich man and Lazarus is one of his most alarming. The dissolute son, on his return, is wined and dined. The rich man lands in a fiery pit. Both end up being toasted — but in very different senses!

Yet the two stories have elements in common. Both speak of God's mercy. The first story illustrates God's mercy toward sinners, the second his mercy toward the destitute and the sick. God loves Lazarus, so he reverses his situation, lifting him up from lying hungry on the ground and placing him next to Abraham at the heavenly banquet ("by his side" — verse 23 — indicates they are reclining at a banquet table together).

In both stories a character faces a choice about showing mercy. The older son had to choose whether to share his father's mercy toward the wayward brother, the rich man whether to extend mercy to Lazarus.

The stories offer images of the consequences of refusing to pass on God's mercy to others. It is like standing outside a party, angered rather than pleased at the sound of the music. It is like being burned. These are only images, of course, not literal descriptions. But they are to be taken seriously as insights into the unhappiness awaiting us if we fail to participate in the mercy that God is showing in the world.

Did the wealthy man deliberately ignore Lazarus's suffering? Apparently. When he notices Lazarus next to Abraham, he already knows his name (verse 24). How could he not know him? Day after day Lazarus lay "at his gate" — right outside his front door (verse 20).

Was the rich man totally self-centered — a reclusive miser who cared for no one but himself? Probably not. Most likely he was a respectable, substantial member of society. Presumably he did not feast every day all alone (verse 19). His table would have been crowded with respectable, substantial people like him — people in a position to do him favors, whose good opinion it was useful to have. In the first-century world, people gained a good reputation by being benefactors, so the rich man may even have been generous — to those who could do things for him in return. But generosity to Lazarus would have seemed pointless. Lazarus was a nobody. He could never do the rich man any favors; his appreciation would not add luster to the rich man's reputation. In one sense Lazarus was close to the rich man — just outside the door. In another sense he was a million miles away.

And that is just how Lazarus appears to the rich man after death (verse 23). In earthly life the rich man put an unbridgeable distance between himself and Lazarus. After death he will remain forever at that unbridgeable distance (verse 26). And since Lazarus has arrived in heaven (represented by Abraham), being at an infinite distance from Lazarus means being at an infinite distance from God.

Jesus tells the story of the rich man and Lazarus to illustrate the effect that wealth can have on a person. In Jesus' view money is not passive or neutral; it is a force that competes with God for our loyalty (verse 13). Money exerts a powerful influence over us. If we let ourselves be dominated by it, it will close our hearts to God.

Of course, we may not notice how love of money is deadening our receptivity to God. But the effect is reflected in something we *can* see: our relationship with people in need. Compassion toward other people reflects an openness to God. Conversely, the rich man's failure to take notice of Lazarus at his door betokened his blindness toward God — a blindness brought on by his devotion to wealth. Love of money rendered him blind to both Lazarus and God.

For Jesus the issue is not how much money we have but how much control our money exercises over us (verse 13). To what degree does pursuing and enjoying material things consume us? To what degree do we expend our money — and time — on people who are in need? Jesus does not provide a formula for determining how well we are doing. He presents the issue squarely — love of God or love of money? love of the needy or love of self? — and leaves us to examine ourselves and make our decisions. Hopefully we will choose more wisely than the rich man in the parable!

Questions for Application

40 minutes
Choose questions according to your interest and time.

1 Who is the Lazarus at your doorstep? at your church's doorstep? at your city's doorstep? at your country's doorstep?

2 As a group, make a list of the obstacles that get in the way of using your time and money to meet other people's needs (for example, being too busy with work, not knowing a suitable organization to support or volunteer with, being on a limited budget). What could you do to overcome at least one of these obstacles in order to be more generous with your talents or resources?

3 How is this reading challenging you to make a change in your life? What concrete action is it leading you to take?

4 The rich man saw Lazarus's suffering without caring enough to help him. Do you find any of that callous attitude in yourself? If so, what concrete step could you take to overcome it?

5 How could you support one another in responding to this reading? What might you be able to do as a group to respond to this reading?

6 The story ends by addressing the problem of knowing God's will but failing to respond to it. Why do we sometimes do that? Where is this a problem in your life?

In a good discussion group, "participants help to clarify one another's comments and question each other for deeper reflection."

Barbara J. Fleischer, *Facilitating for Growth*

Approach to Prayer

15 minutes
Use one of these approaches — or create your own!

✦ Share brief updates on the needs of members of the group that you have been praying for. Have each person pray again for the person to the right, renewing the petition for God's help or thanking him for his response.

Anyone who wishes may offer a spontaneous prayer in response to the reading.

Concluding prayer: "Lord Jesus, give me eyes to see those in need and a heart to have compassion. Help me come to the aid of the needy as you did. Make me a channel of your mercy. Help me not to treat money and possessions as more important than other people."

✦ Pray Psalms 111 and 112, which speak of divine generosity and human generosity. If there are four or more of you, divide into two groups and pray the verses alternately. Conclude each psalm with a Glory to the Father, and end the time with an Our Father.

Saints in the Making

A Life-Changing Story

This section is a supplement for individual reading.

In 1905, at the age of thirty, Albert Schweitzer had achieved recognition as both a theologian and a professional organist. Yet he was unsettled about his future. When he read a magazine article appealing for European doctors to meet the desperate need for medical care in central Africa, Schweitzer knew what he must do. He left his promising dual careers and put himself through medical school. In 1913, after raising funds, Schweitzer set up a clinic on the Ogowe River in present-day Gabon. Except for an interruption caused by World War I, he worked there until his death in 1965.

In a 1924 book, Schweitzer explained the thinking that led to his decision:

I read about the physical miseries of the natives in the virgin forests. And the more I thought about it, the stranger it seemed to me that we Europeans trouble ourselves so little about the great humanitarian task which offers itself to us. The parable of Dives* and Lazarus seemed to me to have been spoken directly at us! We are Dives, for, through the advances of medical science, we now know a great deal about disease and pain, and have innumerable means of fighting them. Out there in the colonies, however, sits wretched Lazarus, the coloured folk, who suffers from illness and pain just as much as we do, nay, much more, and has absolutely no means of fighting them. And just as Dives sinned against the poor man at his gate because, for want of thought, he never put himself in his place and let his heart and conscience tell him what he ought to do, so do we sin against the poor man at our gate.

---

* The unnamed wealthy man in Jesus' parable in Luke 16 is sometimes called Dives, the Latin word for *rich.*

Between Discussions

In our second reading we saw Jesus invite a tax collector named Levi to become one of his disciples. In other sections of Luke, Jesus invites a good number of men and women to be disciples.

Jesus' specific words to Levi were "Follow me" (5:27). Jesus spent his days walking from village to village. He did not have a training facility or even a settled residence. Thus being his disciple meant literally following him. For this reason, Jesus' disciples had to leave everyone and everything behind. Peter and Andrew could hardly take their boat along as they followed Jesus to the next town.

At the same time, Jesus had others who were devoted to him whom he did not call to follow him as disciples. They were part of the restored community of God that he was gathering around him. But they stayed at home, rather than following him along the roads of Galilee.

Luke wrote some decades after Jesus' death and resurrection. In Luke's day it had become possible for everyone who believed in Jesus to be a disciple because, as risen Lord, he was now always present by the Spirit in the whole Christian community. On the other hand, it was impossible for anyone literally to follow Jesus, since his touring of Galilee had come to an end.

Apparently, however, Luke thought that *following* remained a useful way of speaking about being a disciple for Luke structured his Gospel to emphasize the picture of Jesus traveling along the road with his disciples. Drawing on the tradition of apostolic preaching, Luke incorporated considerable material in his Gospel that the other Gospel writers did not use, and he inserted much of it into Jesus' journey to Jerusalem (chapters 9–19). As a result, in Luke's narrative much of Jesus' ministry takes place on the road. Luke's intention, it seems, was to show that being a disciple of Jesus continues to involve the sorts of things that the first disciples experienced as they followed him: spending time with him, paying attention to what he does, having their lives drawn toward the destiny that he was traveling to in Jerusalem—his passage from death into risen life.

If disciples of Jesus still follow, they must also, in some way, leave behind. Divesting oneself of one's possessions and giving to the needy continue as features of discipleship because Jesus draws us into an intimate, trusting relationship with God as Father. To trust in the real God, we have to stop trusting in the false god money. Our efforts to dethrone this false god necessarily involve some relinquishment. Moreover, the disciple imitates the master. Jesus has come to show mercy to the needy, so we show mercy too.

Just as Jesus did not ask all his first friends to leave home and follow him on the road, so he does not intend all his later followers to give away all their possessions — although this option is available through joining a religious order. But Jesus does call all of us to dethrone the false god money and use our resources and talents to help meet the needs of the poor.

Jesus makes this point through a parable about a wealthy farmer who stands as the opposite of what a disciple should be. The man trusts in money, and he uses his money in an individualistic way, not recognizing any responsibility to the community (12:13 – 21). According to Jesus, this man is a "fool" (12:20).

Jesus declares that God's kingdom will reverse the condition of the poor. This is one message of the parable of the rich man and Lazarus. Jesus offers a further image of this reversal in a parable of a host who gives a great banquet. When the wealthy people whom he invites decline to attend, he fills the house with beggars and other social misfits (14:15 – 24).

But this reversal in the situation of the poor is not reserved entirely for the age to come. By his miraculous healings and provision of food, Jesus shows that God is already beginning to reverse the condition of the needy in the *present* world. Jesus intends the prospect of a future reversal of poverty to inspire his disciples' actions here and now. When you yourselves give a dinner party, Jesus says, invite beggars and other social misfits (see 14:12 – 14). Thus Jesus tells the story of the rich man and Lazarus to spur his stay-at-home disciples to do what the rich man failed to do — care for the needy person on the doorstep.

You Will Be
with Me in Paradise

Questions to Begin

15 minutes
Use a question or two to get warmed up for the reading.

---

1 What's your approach to farewells?
   ❏ Keep it short and sweet.
   ❏ I try to say good-bye to each person.
   ❏ I like a hug.
   ❏ It can take hours (sometimes the most interesting conversations happen when you're saying good-bye!).
   ❏ I'd rather not say good-bye.

---

2 What is the single most memorable meal you have ever had? Why do you remember it so well?

---

3 When have you joined in making fun of someone — and later regretted it?

Opening the Bible

5 minutes
Have someone in the group read "The Reading" aloud. (If par-
ticipants have not already read "What's Happened," read it aloud
also. Otherwise skip it.)

What's Happened

Jesus' lengthy journey to Jerusalem has ended. He has arrived in Jerusalem at the time of the Passover celebration.

Thousands of pilgrims have crowded into the city for the feast. Many have arrived a week before the feast begins in order to undergo a period of ritual purification. Jesus chooses this time, when the city is filled with crowds, to perform a sensational symbolic action in the temple, driving out some of the people who were carrying on business that was necessary for the temple to function (19:45–48). His action is an attempt to clear away commercial activities in the temple. But Jesus seems to be indicating that, now that he has come on the scene, the temple will no longer play a central role in God's relationship with his people. This brings Jesus into conflict with the priests in charge of the temple.

Jesus teaches publicly in the temple by day and on a nearby hillside with his disciples in the evenings. Meanwhile the temple authorities plot to arrest him and have him killed. Knowing what is afoot, Jesus shares a final meal with his inner circle of disciples.

The Reading: Luke 22:14–20, 24–30; 23:32–43

A Final Meal with Friends

14 When the hour came, he took his place at the table, and the apostles with him. 15 He said to them, "I have eagerly desired to eat this Passover with you before I suffer; 16 for I tell you, I will not eat it until it is fulfilled in the kingdom of God." 17 Then he took a cup, and after giving thanks he said, "Take this and divide it among yourselves; 18 for I tell you that from now on I will not drink of the fruit of the vine until the kingdom of God comes."

19 Then he took a loaf of bread, and when he had given thanks, he broke it and gave it to them, saying, "This is my body, which is given for you. Do this in remembrance of me." 20 And he did the same with the cup after supper, saying, "This cup that is poured out for you is the new covenant in my blood." . . .

^{24} A dispute also arose among them as to which one of them was to be regarded as the greatest. ^{25} But he said to them, "The kings of the Gentiles lord it over them; and those in authority over them are called benefactors. ^{26} But not so with you; rather the greatest among you must become like the youngest, and the leader like one who serves. ^{27} For who is greater, the one who is at the table or the one who serves? Is it not the one at the table? But I am among you as one who serves.

^{28} "You are those who have stood by me in my trials; ^{29} and I confer on you, just as my Father has conferred on me, a kingdom, ^{30} so that you may eat and drink at my table in my kingdom." . . .

The King and the Convict

23:32 Two others also, who were criminals, were led away to be put to death with him. ^{33} When they came to the place that is called The Skull, they crucified Jesus there with the criminals, one on his right and one on his left. ^{34} Then Jesus said, "Father, forgive them; for they do not know what they are doing." And they cast lots to divide his clothing.

^{35} And the people stood by, watching; but the leaders scoffed at him, saying, "He saved others; let him save himself if he is the Messiah of God, his chosen one!" ^{36} The soldiers also mocked him, coming up and offering him sour wine, ^{37} and saying, "If you are the King of the Jews, save yourself!" ^{38} There was also an inscription over him, "This is the King of the Jews."

^{39} One of the criminals who were hanged there kept deriding him and saying, "Are you not the Messiah? Save yourself and us!" ^{40} But the other rebuked him, saying, "Do you not fear God, since you are under the same sentence of condemnation? ^{41} And we indeed have been condemned justly, for we are getting what we deserve for our deeds, but this man has done nothing wrong." ^{42} Then he said, "Jesus, remember me when you come into your kingdom." ^{43} He replied, "Truly I tell you, today you will be with me in Paradise."

Questions for Careful Reading

10 minutes
Choose questions according to your interest and time.

1 What role does 22:27 suggest Jesus played at the Last Supper?

2 What qualities of a good teacher does Jesus display in 22:25–27? What do you suppose he was feeling?

3 Jesus directs his followers to keep on celebrating his last meal "in remembrance" of him (22:19). Do any of Jesus' statements suggest that celebrating the Lord's Supper should point our attention not only toward the past but also toward the future?

4 The second criminal undergoes a last-minute conversion (23:40–42). What elements of conversion can you discover in what he says?

A Guide to the Reading

If participants have not read this section already, read it aloud. Otherwise go on to "Questions for Application."

In our readings so far, Jesus has announced by word and deed that God's kingdom is about to arrive. God's kingdom is a powerful reality — his loving care breaking into human lives. Jesus' healing of the sick and his socializing with sinners have already given people a taste of God's kingdom (Week 2). His parables have illustrated the essential mercy of the kingdom: the father of the two sons modeled God's forgiveness (Week 3) and the heavenly comfort Lazarus received reflected God's compassion for the poor (Week 4). Now Jesus secures our access to God's kingdom — at the price of his own suffering and death.

The two scenes that we read are taken from Luke's account of Jesus' final hours. We read of Jesus' last meal and his execution, omitting the account in between of his arrest, interrogation, and condemnation. It is appropriate to set the scenes at the table and at the cross side by side, like two photos in one of those hinged double frames, for the meal and the death have the closest possible connection.

Jesus' death coincides with the great Jewish feast of Passover. Passover celebrates the Israelites' exodus, or going out, from slavery in Egypt. Now it will be Jesus who goes out, leaving this world by a painful death to enter into the majesty of God (9:28 – 31). Thereby he will bring God's kingdom to men and women (notice how Jesus connects his suffering with the coming of the kingdom in 22:15 – 18).

Using words that echo Old Testament passages on sacrifice, Jesus indicates what his death will accomplish: his body will be given, his blood poured out, to form a new covenant, a bond, between God and human beings (22:19 – 20). How Jesus' death brings this about is a mystery that even the greatest saints and theologians can never fully penetrate. Jesus simply tells his disciples simply that in God's plan it "must" be (9:22; 17:25; 22:37).

By using the Passover meal to explain the purpose of his death, Jesus refocuses the meal on himself. With the words "do this in remembrance of me" (22:19), Jesus re-creates the Passover meal as the sacrament of his presence. He speaks new words at the breaking of bread before the meal and at the blessing of wine afterward. Of the bread he declares, "This is my body, which is given for you"; of the cup, "This cup that is poured out for you is the new covenant in my blood" (22:19–20).

Thus through all ages, Jesus' saving death will continue to be present to his followers in this meal, because he himself will be fully, truly present. Jesus is so present in the Eucharist, in fact, that when we celebrate it, we do not merely remember or repeat the Last Supper: we become participants in it. Comparing the altar in the church to the table of the Last Supper, St. John Chrysostom, the fourth-century bishop, declared, "This table is the same as that, and nothing less."

The scene shifts to just outside the city, to a small outcropping of rock called, because of its shape, the Skull (*Golgotha* in Aramaic, *Calvary* in Latin — 23:33). Jesus had justified his friendships with transgressors as an expression of God's open invitation to be reconciled with him. At the Skull, Jesus continues this mission to his last breath, spending his final hours among criminals.

The religious leaders, the execution squad, and one of the criminals hanging next to Jesus ridicule him (23:35–37, 39). They assume that if the Messiah were mistreated, he would save himself. They do not understand that the Messiah has come not to save himself but to save others.

Who can say how much the other criminal understands? But at least he has the humility to acknowledge his sins and his need for Jesus and to put his trust in Jesus at the moment when Jesus appears least able to help anyone. Somehow the repentant convict perceives that the titles others are using to mock Jesus — "king," "Messiah" (23:35–39) — are true. Jesus really *is* the king sent by God (23:42).

When the convict appeals to Jesus to have mercy on him, the dying king gives him the assurance that we hope to hear at the hour of our death (23:43). In fact, Jesus' conversation with the man expresses the ultimate purpose of Jesus' life and death: to forge the way for men and women to receive God's forgiveness, to secure a place for us at the joyous supper in the kingdom (22:30). To share that supper is the ultimate purpose of our lives.

Questions for Application

40 minutes
Choose questions according to your interest and time.

1 Jesus was under a great deal of stress at the Last Supper. What was Jesus' focus during this last meal with his friends? What stresses in your family surface during meals? What could you learn from Jesus' example?

2 The disciples do not seem to grasp the seriousness of the moment or Jesus' call to serve (22:24). When have you failed to grasp the seriousness of a moment or an opportunity to serve? What is Jesus calling you to do through Luke 22:26?

3 Do you think it was easy for Jesus to pray for forgiveness for his enemies (23:34)? Is there a situation in which you might imitate him?

4 In baptism and the creed, Christians affirm that Jesus gave his life for us. Have you affirmed this for yourself? If you believe that Jesus did what is described in this reading for you, what adjustments should you make in your life to respond to his love?

5 People have diverse responses to contemplating Jesus on the cross. What feelings do you have as you read about the crucifixion?

6 In what way can the repentant criminal's response to Jesus suggest the response you might make to him?

"Calling members after a missed meeting to communicate the next meeting-date and the assigned home enables participants to maintain continuity and feel wanted within the group."

Dianne and Roger Miller, *Meeting Christ in Scripture*

Approach to Prayer

15 minutes
Use this approach — or create your own!

+ Begin with this prayer: "Lord Jesus, like the repentant thief, I have nothing to offer you except my repentance and my faith in you. Like him, I appeal to you. Have mercy and remember me this day in your kingdom. Lord Jesus, you have given your life for me. Help me respond to you with my whole life."

  Allow an opportunity for anyone to express to the Lord — silently or aloud — the thoughts that are on their mind after the reading and discussion.

  Finally pray together Psalm 22, a prayer that foreshadowed Jesus' death. According to the Gospels of Matthew and Mark, he prayed it on the cross.

A Living Tradition

The Repentant Thief

This section is a supplement for individual reading.

Here is the model of conversion that we should aim at, since forgiveness is instantly lavished on the thief, and he finds favor and friendship more abundant than he asked for — because the Lord always bestows more than we request. The thief asked the Lord to remember him when he came into his kingdom, but the Lord said, "I assure you, today you will be with me in paradise." For life consists in being with Christ, because where Christ is, there is the kingdom. The reason the Lord pardoned the man so quickly was that the man so quickly turned to him.

St. Ambrose of Milan

The thief acknowledged his sin, testified to Christ's innocence, believed in him, addressed him as king even though he was hanging on a cross. By all this he snatched for himself the inheritance of the saints.

St. Cyril of Alexandria

My patron saints are those who have stolen heaven — like the good thief. The great saints have earned heaven by their works; as for me, I will imitate the thief, I will have it by ruse, a ruse of love, which will open heaven's gates to me and to poor sinners.

St. Thérèse of Lisieux

Accept me as a partaker of your mystical supper, O Son of God, for I will not reveal your mystery to your enemies, nor will I give you a kiss as did Judas, but like the thief I confess to you: Remember me, O Lord, when you come into your kingdom! Remember me, O Master, when you come into your kingdom! Remember me, O Holy One, when you come into your kingdom! May the partaking of your holy mysteries, O Lord, be not for my judgment or condemnation, but for the healing of soul and body.

Pre-communion prayer of the Byzantine liturgy

Between Discussions

L uke's description of the Last Supper and Jesus' crucifixion gives us much food for thought. Here are two lines of reflection, one concerning the Eucharist, the other concerning the sacrament of reconciliation:

The Eucharist. The Passover meal was, and is, a celebration of God's saving mercy. The meal thanks God in the normal Old Testament manner by remembering God's saving actions, praising him for what he has done, and telling other people about it. The Passover meal specifically recalls how God rescued the Israelites from backbreaking toil and genocidal oppression in Egypt. At various moments before and during the meal there are blessings in connection with wine and bread. It is not the food that is blessed, however, but God: God is blessed, that is, praised, over the food. So the whole meal is an expression of praise and thanks to God for his saving acts. The final blessing over the wine adds a prayer of petition for the welfare of God's people, Israel.

Luke does not describe the entire Passover meal that Jesus ate with his disciples but records only the words by which Jesus gave the meal new meaning. In their liturgy, however, the early Christians did not merely repeat these few words of Jesus. They celebrated a Christian adaptation of the Passover meal — a festive meal with prayers of praise and thanksgiving to God for his saving deeds. But instead of recalling the exodus, they gave thanks for the death and resurrection of Jesus, which bring freedom from sin and death. In addition, they offered prayers of petition for God's people, the Church.

Eventually the meal was dropped, but the prayers remained. While the form of the Eucharist evolved, the original elements continued to provide the underlying structure. The eucharistic prayer today begins with praise and thanks to God for his goodness, above all for his ultimate saving deed, the death and resurrection of his Son. It quotes the words of institution by which Jesus gave the meal its new meaning centered on himself. And it concludes with prayers on behalf of God's people, the Church.

Seeing the connection between the Passover meal that Jesus celebrated before he died and the liturgy that we celebrate today helps us understand why the liturgical celebration is called the Eucharist. The word *eucharist* comes from the Greek for "thanksgiving." The Christian liturgy is an act of thanksgiving because, ever since its origin in the Passover meal, it praises and thanks God for his ultimate saving action through Jesus.

The next time you are at Mass, pay attention to the eucharistic prayer (it begins with the exchange "Lift up your hearts," "We lift them up to the Lord"). Notice how the prayer is the great proclamation of thanks and praise to God for the saving action of his Son and the great prayer for the Church and the world. Do you actively take part in the whole celebration? Do you weave your heart and your voice into the responses and songs that make up the fabric of the Eucharist?

The sacrament of reconciliation. Jesus provoked harsh criticism by dining with tax collectors and sinners. The Gospel of Luke shows that Jesus' disciples were also a deeply flawed group of individuals. For example, they were divided by rivalrous ambitions (9:46; 22:24). Thus throughout his life Jesus sought out the company of men and women who were far from holy.

Jesus' showed his affection for imperfect people quite clearly at his final meal. He dined with faithless followers. One would betray him (22:21–22). Another would deny him (22:31–34). The rest would humiliate him by abandoning him. Yet Jesus told them, "I have eagerly desired to eat this Passover with you before I suffer" (22:15). His deeply felt love for people was not diminished by their failings, even when their failings added to his suffering.

Jesus' final hours were the proving ground of his love. Shame and torture would have ripped the veneer of niceness off any latent vengefulness. But at his crucifixion Jesus asked God to forgive those who were putting him to death (23:34). He was a man of mercy through and through.

Is this the Jesus you picture as you come to the sacrament of reconciliation?

THE LORD HAS RISEN INDEED

Questions to Begin

15 minutes
Use a question or two to get warmed up for the reading.

1 Two disciples in this reading walk fourteen miles in a day. What is your response to the suggestion of walking fourteen miles in a day?

❑ No problem. (Hey, I run that far.)

❑ Sounds like a decent hike — if I were in shape.

❑ I enjoy walking. But not fourteen miles!

❑ Walking is best with a friend.

❑ I wish!

2 Has anyone said something to you recently that lifted you out of discouragement?

3 What was your most interesting conversation with a stranger while traveling?

4 How has entertaining strangers had unexpected benefits for you?

5 minutes
Have someone in the group read "The Reading" aloud. (If participants have not already read "What's Happened," read it aloud also. Otherwise skip it.)

What's Happened

Jesus hangs crucified for some time after speaking with the repentant criminal. Then, quoting a psalm, he cries out, "Father, into your hands I commend my spirit," and dies (23:46). Thus Jesus ends his life as he began it, calling God his Father and giving himself completely to his Father's purposes (2:49).

Several women who are followers of Jesus have stood off at a distance, watching him die. They continue to watch as one of Jesus' friends removes his body from the cross and places it in a tomb hewn out of a rock hillside. The women wish to dignify Jesus' burial with aromatic spices. But because it is late Friday afternoon and the Sabbath is about to begin, they return to their lodgings and observe the Jewish day of rest. As soon as they can on Sunday morning, however, they go back to the tomb where they saw Jesus' body laid, bringing the spices. To their astonishment, the tomb is empty.

Two men — evidently angels — appear and reproach the women for seeking "the living among the dead" (24:4–5). The angels remind the women that Jesus predicted both his death and his resurrection.

The women are terrified. They go to tell the male disciples what they have seen and heard. The men dismiss the women's report as nonsense, although Peter goes to investigate and discovers that the tomb is, in fact, empty.

The Reading: Luke 24:13–35

On the Road and at Table with Jesus Once Again

13 Now on that same day two of them were going to a village called Emmaus, about seven miles from Jerusalem, 14 and talking with each other about all these things that had happened. 15 While they were talking and discussing, Jesus himself came near and went with them, 16 but their eyes were kept from recognizing him.

17 And he said to them, "What are you discussing with each other while you walk along?"

They stood still, looking sad. 18 Then one of them, whose name was Cleopas, answered him, "Are you the only stranger in Jerusalem who does not know the things that have taken place there in these days?"

19 He asked them, "What things?"

They replied, "The things about Jesus of Nazareth, who was a prophet mighty in deed and word before God and all the people, 20 and how our chief priests and leaders handed him over to be condemned to death and crucified him. 21 But we had hoped that he was the one to redeem Israel. Yes, and besides all this, it is now the third day since these things took place. 22 Moreover, some women of our group astounded us. They were at the tomb early this morning, 23 and when they did not find his body there, they came back and told us that they had indeed seen a vision of angels who said that he was alive. 24 Some of those who were with us went to the tomb and found it just as the women had said; but they did not see him."

25 Then he said to them, "Oh, how foolish you are, and how slow of heart to believe all that the prophets have declared! 26 Was it not necessary that the Messiah should suffer these things and then enter into his glory?" 27 Then beginning with Moses and all the prophets, he interpreted to them the things about himself in all the scriptures.

28 As they came near the village to which they were going, he walked ahead as if he were going on. 29 But they urged him strongly, saying, "Stay with us, because it is almost evening and the day is now nearly over." So he went in to stay with them.

30 When he was at the table with them, he took bread, blessed and broke it, and gave it to them. 31 Then their eyes were opened, and they recognized him; and he vanished from their sight.

32 They said to each other, "Were not our hearts burning within us while he was talking to us on the road, while he was opening the scriptures to us?"

33 That same hour they got up and returned to Jerusalem; and they found the eleven and their companions gathered together. 34 They were saying, "The Lord has risen indeed, and he has appeared to Simon!" 35 Then they told what had happened on the road, and how he had been made known to them in the breaking of the bread.

10 minutes
Choose questions according to your interest and time.

1 Jesus seems to play ignorant in verse 19. Why?

2 Compare verse 30 with the description of the Last Supper in the previous reading (22:14, 19). What similarities can you detect?

3 What does verse 32 suggest about what the disciples had experienced with Jesus in the past?

4 From glimpses of Jesus' disciples in this reading (especially in verses 13 – 15, 22 – 24, 33 – 35), what picture do you get of their relationships with one another?

5 Some people allege that Jesus' disciples manufactured the story of his resurrection. What evidence against this theory can you find in the reading? (Consider verses 1 – 12 also.)

A Guide to the Reading

If participants have not read this section already, read it aloud. Otherwise go on to "Questions for Application."

On the Sunday following Jesus' death, two of his followers are walking from Jerusalem to a neighboring village, probably their hometown. A second-century tradition identified Cleopas (verse 18) as a brother of Joseph, Jesus' foster father. A son of Cleopas later became a leader of the church in Jerusalem. Some scholars suggest that the unnamed companion is Cleopas's wife.

We can gauge the darkness of the two disciples' depression from the brightness of their now-shattered expectations for Jesus (verses 19 – 21). They had thought they were on the brink of God's decisive saving action in the world — only to see his specially designated agent destroyed by a ghastly execution.

Jesus comes up to the pair as they walk along, but they do not recognize him. On other occasions after his resurrection Jesus' disciples also fail to recognize him at first (Matthew 28:17; John 20:14). This is probably due to the inconceivable transformation he has undergone.

Jesus tells the pair squarely that they do not understand God's plan (verse 25). In a way, they are as misguided as the people who taunted Jesus at the cross. The mockers thought the Messiah would use heavenly power to save himself; it was totally contrary to their thinking that the Messiah would accomplish his work of healing and reconciling by means of suffering and death. Yet, Jesus explains to his two followers, it was precisely God's plan to work through a suffering Messiah — a plan God had sketched out beforehand in Scripture (verses 26 – 27).

We may assume that as they walked along Jesus also set the disciples straight regarding their expectation that he would liberate Israel (verse 21). Jesus *is* the savior of Israel, but not of Israel alone, and not from its political enemies. He has come forth from Israel to save both Jews and non-Jews from sin in all its devastating forms and to share with all people his own resurrection from death.

For the two disciples, these are revolutionary views. Little in Judaism at the time has led them to expect that the Messiah would enter the splendor of God's presence by way of suffering. For us today the idea of a suffering Messiah — a crucified Christ — is perhaps all too familiar. But does familiarity make it any easier to grasp or respond to? How astonishing that God would bring his mercy to us through his Son's humiliating torment! And how unpalatable are the implications, for we can follow the suffering Messiah into his glory only by taking the road of humility, service, and suffering with him (see 9:23–27). Shaping our lives to the model of the suffering Messiah is a lifetime challenge (we may recall the difficulty the first disciples had taking hold of this message; for example, see 22:24–27).

After the stranger lays out such an astounding explanation of God's plan of salvation, it is no wonder the disciples ask him to stay for dinner (verse 29). Then a reversal of roles occurs. The guest plays the part of the host: Jesus says the blessing over the bread (verse 30), and the disciples recognize him. Immediately he vanishes (verse 31).

The two disciples have learned more from the afternoon's events than the bare fact that Jesus is risen. His explanation on the road has helped them understand that suffering has been his path into splendor and authority with God. By the timing of their recognition of him, he showed them how he will continue to be with them: they know him at the moment he repeats the action he performed at the Last Supper. This action lies at the center of the meal he has told his apostles to repeat, the meal that will make present his sacrificial death (compare verse 30 with 22:14, 19). In this meal, he had declared, the bread and wine would become his body and blood (22:19–20). By his appearance at the meal at Emmaus, Jesus reveals the fulfillment of that promise. He shows that in the celebration of this meal he will continue to accompany his disciples and provide the strength they need to make their way into his glory.

Significantly, Luke does not say that Jesus left but that he "vanished from their sight" (verse 31). The point of the story is that, though Jesus is invisible, in the celebration of the Eucharist he remains with us in a way more real than we can understand.

Questions for Application

40 minutes
Choose questions according to your interest and time.

1 What is your understanding of the purpose of Jesus' death and resurrection? If Jesus has truly passed through suffering and death into risen life, what implications does this have for your life?

2 What do verses 25–27, and 32 suggest about the purpose and experience of Scripture in the life of Jesus' disciples today? ("Moses and all the prophets" —verse 27—refers to what Christians call the Old Testament.) What place does Scripture have in your life?

3 What elements of faith are you sometimes slow to believe (see verse 25)? What might you do to strengthen your faith?

4 What area of discouragement do you face? Does this reading say anything to you about it?

5 How has the Lord shown you the reality of his presence? What effect did this experience have on you? What effect does it have on you now?

6 What is the most important thing you are going to take away from these readings and discussions of Luke? What is the most important response to Jesus that Luke's Gospel invites you to make?

"Sometimes my first response to a question is a 'shallow' one. I work to find a better, deeper answer."

Norma Spande, *Your Guide to Successful Home Bible Studies*

Approach to Prayer

15 minutes
Use this approach — or create your own!

✦ Opening prayer: "We thank you, Lord Jesus, for your presence with us during our reading and discussions. Thank you for your words to us, which you have spoken to us by your Spirit, through the Gospel and through one another. Help us respond to the words you have spoken to each of us. Lord, let it be done to us according to your word!"

Give everyone an opportunity to offer a brief, spontaneous prayer expressing their response to what God has given them through the readings and discussions.

End by praying Mary's prayer together (1:46–55).

Saints in the Making

Luke's First Readers

This section is a supplement for individual reading.

With one exception (see 1:3), we do not know the names of Luke's first readers. But at least a few of them seem to have been materially well off. Luke's literary style is, in places, quite refined—designed for people who have had the leisure, and thus the resources, to obtain a decent education. Luke preserves many sayings of Jesus that are particularly aimed at people who have some wealth (for example, the story of the rich man and Lazarus).

People of lower social standing also belonged to the early Christian communities, and some of them undoubtedly were very poor. There were slaves and, materially even worse off, free unskilled laborers, who were hired one day at a time and earned enough to live on for the next day. If one day they did not get work, the next day they did not eat.

Raised in a pagan culture that had little concern for the poor, the wealthy Christians may not have been inclined toward generosity with their poorer brothers and sisters. (First Corinthians 11:17–22 offers evidence of such a problem.) But many well-off converts to Christianity *did* learn a new way of relating to the poor. The writings of the early church make many references to the regular collections taken up for widows, orphans, and the elderly.

Moreover, in Luke's time the Eucharist was still celebrated in the context of an actual meal at the home of a community member affluent enough to provide space for a meeting. Historian Philip F. Esler writes, "It was virtually unknown . . . for representatives from the top and from the bottom of the social hierarchy to gather together in a single association" as happened in the Christian Eucharist.

Thus, Esler writes, those people from the upper strata of society who tried to live the gospel as Luke presented it gave away not only some of their money but also some of their social respectability. The Christians who were willing to follow Jesus this way were, indeed, saints in the making.

After Words

It is difficult to leave our discussion of Emmaus without a few additional reflections.

On the road to Emmaus, Jesus explains Scripture to the disciples, showing how it points to him. Then he breaks bread with them. Luke's readers would immediately have seen in these actions a parallel to their celebration of the Eucharist, in which reading of and preaching on Scripture was followed by prayers and communion with the risen Lord in the consecrated bread and wine. Since our eucharistic celebration today still consists of a liturgy of the Word and a liturgy of the Eucharist, the parallel with Emmaus is equally clear. Our Christian worship is grounded in Jesus' actions with his disciples at Emmaus. Indeed, it is a continuation of Jesus' actions. Every time we celebrate the Eucharist, we share in Jesus' meal at Emmaus, just as we share in the Last Supper.

There are, in fact, a number of connections between the Last Supper and the Emmaus meal. At the Last Supper, Jesus commissioned his disciples to celebrate a meal remembering his saving death, a meal through which he would continue to be present with them in the bread and the wine. At Emmaus, after explaining his saving death, Jesus shows his disciples that he is indeed with them in the breaking of the bread. The Last Supper was a farewell before departure; the Emmaus meal was a resumption of life together, a "remaining with" meal.

If we put these two meals together with other meals in Luke and the Acts of the Apostles (which Luke also wrote), we see that they are part of a larger pattern. There is a series of meals leading up to Jesus' death and resurrection, then a series of meals following his death and resurrection. The pattern looks like this:

✦ From Galilee to Jerusalem Jesus practiced table fellowship with all sorts of men and women, gathering them into a new community of God's people. These meals reached a climax at the Last Supper, when Jesus gave himself to his friends completely in a meal that already made present his saving death and resurrection.

✦ Jesus suffered, died, and rose to new life.

✦ Jesus celebrated a kind of First Supper with his friends at Emmaus. In this meal he made his crucified and glorified self present to them. This new meal now continues on in Christian celebrations of the Eucharist, in which Jesus gathers all sorts of men and women into a renewed community of God's people centered on himself. Here is where we fit in. As we join in the Eucharist, we hear Jesus teach and we dine with him, like the disciples at Emmaus. We have access to his mercy as did the people who approached him when he was traveling from town to town in Galilee and sharing meals with them.

The celebration of the Lord's Supper will stretch on to the end of time, when the kingdom of God comes fully. And our celebration makes us participants not only in the past events of Jesus' death and resurrection but also in this future fulfillment. Jesus spoke of God's kingdom as a great banquet (14:15 – 24). He linked his final meal before his death to that ultimate banquet (22:16, 18). Because our eating and drinking in the Eucharist is communion with the crucified one who already reigns with God, our eating and drinking is already a sharing in the Final Supper of his kingdom that will come.

The introduction to this booklet raised the question "How well do I know myself?" Now, at the end of Luke, we might return to this question. What happiness are we seeking? Would we be happy if we attained it? Do we know what will really make us happy?

Luke shows us that sharing in God's happiness means being transformed into people oriented toward the happiness of others. Truly receiving God's mercy means being remade into people who show mercy. Are we willing to undergo that transformation?

Mercy and More Mercy

Of all the teachers I had in grade school, the one I remember most happily is Sister Inez Raymond. As a boy I got into conflict with a number of teachers, largely because I disliked authority. But I don't recall ever crossing swords with Sister Inez. The reason, I think, was that she liked me too much. And it was not favoritism: she liked all of us. Her genuine fondness for us junior high students was, in fact, her outstanding feature.

Yet Sister Inez did not have a rowdy class. We respected her. More than other teachers she used games to make learning fun, but she was serious about our learning. Sister Inez had a high estimate of what we were capable of, and she did not rest until we achieved it. Her individual affection for each student made it hard to escape her searching attention. Hers was not a class where you could easily hide your lack of effort in the crowd.

I suspect most of us have a Sister Inez or two in our past— a teacher who combined deep kindness with high expectations. As I read the Gospel of Luke, I am led to think that Jesus was something like Sister Inez—or that she was a little like him (as Sister Inez would say, if that modest woman could be brought to acknowledge any resemblance between herself and Jesus). Luke shows us Jesus being merciful to a seemingly reckless degree, yet at the same time making virtually impossible demands on people. Seeing this paradox on a small scale in people like Sister Inez may help us grasp how Jesus could display these apparently irreconcilable characteristics.

A significant demonstration of Jesus' mercy was his practice of dining in the homes of "tax collectors and sinners." Twice in our selected readings people criticize Jesus for this behavior (5:30; 15:2). The reproach followed him through his public life (7:34; 19:7). When we consider who tax collectors and sinners were, the criticism is easy to understand. Tax collectors were not government employees. Tax collection was privatized, as we would say today. The government contracted with independent agents to collect the tolls and backed the collectors with police enforcement. Tax collectors extracted much more from people than they owed the government and kept the difference. Tax collection was institutionalized extortion. The system worked quite well for tax collectors financially — although not socially. Not surprisingly, they were as unpopular as gangsters.

"Sinners" is a broader group. Jews who strictly observed certain portions of the Mosaic law sometimes applied the term *sinners* to Jews who did not keep those portions with the same rigor. But *sinners* also had a more serious application. In the Old Testament the word *sinners* meant "the wicked." The wicked were those who schemed to seize poor people's land, exploited widows and orphans, destroyed others' reputations with malicious slander, even plotted their neighbors' murder (for example, see Psalm 10).

It would have been remarkable for any religious reformer to cultivate friendships with such people. What is particularly astonishing about Jesus' doing so is that he placed a heavy emphasis on mercy to the poor — yet tax collectors and sinners were people who preyed on the poor. Jesus proclaimed good news for the poor and release for the oppressed (4:17 – 21) — yet tax collectors were the very definition of oppressors. Every penny of extra tax they imposed on shipments of flour or dates made food that much more expensive for poor people. Men like Zacchaeus, who became wealthy by manipulating the tax system (19:2, 8), were the exact opposite of the poor whom Jesus proclaimed blessed in the kingdom of God. Jesus' dining behavior was as shocking as would be that of a preacher in the nineteenth-century American South who proclaimed the gospel to slaves in the cotton field, then had dinner at the plantation owner's mansion.

How can we understand Jesus' friendship with both the exploited and their exploiters? It may be that Jesus saw the tax collectors and sinners as also, in some sense, poor. Not that Jesus spiritualized away the meaning of poverty. The Greek word for the poor in Luke's Gospel literally means "beggars," and that is clearly how Jesus intended it. Lazarus was, precisely, a beggar. But alongside material poverty, Jesus recognized impoverishment in relation to God (12:21) and what we might call social impoverishment, or rejection by other people. He felt a deep compassion for those who suffered any kind of poverty. His compassion for the materially poor did not cancel out his compassion for the affluent but spiritually and socially poor people who oppressed them.

Jesus' love for tax collectors and sinners seems to have been deep rooted and long term. There is reason to think that he dined not only with those who repented of their injustices but also with those who did not immediately accept his message. For if Jesus had always succeeded in leading tax collectors to instantly change their ways and make restitution to those they had gouged, his dining with them would probably have won him applause rather than criticism. As historian E. P. Sanders points out, everyone who bought taxed goods would have welcomed the sight of repentant tax collectors. The fact that people continued to carp about Jesus' friendships with tax collectors throughout his public life suggests that he maintained friendships with those who did not immediately repent.

Thus Luke portrays Jesus as a person of limitless mercy. Yet his mercy has nothing to do with a relaxed attitude toward sin. Jesus did not take sin more lightly than his opponents, the Jewish religious leaders. When he explains his program of friendship with sinners, he makes it clear that the heavenly rejoicing over those who return to God commences when they repent (15:7, 10; see 7:36–50). For Jesus, mercy means forgiving sins, not overlooking them or rationalizing them away.

Indeed, Jesus not only maintained the existing standard of righteousness; he raised it. Love even your enemies, he taught (6:27). Deny yourself, take up your cross, and follow me (9:23). Jesus demands more than rule keeping. He asks for perfection.

What does Jesus' paradox of mercy and demand mean for those of us who seek to follow him?

For one thing, we can draw hope from Jesus' ongoing friendships with tax collectors and sinners, for it shows that he loves us without conditions. His love for us is not based on the quality of our lives or the excellence of our present response to his message. He loves us prior to any response we may make, in order to lead us to respond to him. He loves us even when we hesitate to respond, even when we stall.

Furthermore, the perfection Jesus demands is essentially a perfection of mercy. He summons us to become perfect in giving away what he gives to us. He calls us to humble ourselves and take on the role of servant toward others in imitation of him, who humbled himself and became our servant (22:24 – 27).

Finally, we can be encouraged by the glimpse in Luke's Gospel of how Jesus' mercy and his demands came together in his relationship with his disciples. Clearly Jesus summoned them in an utterly uncompromising fashion to a life of forgiveness, mercy, and service. Yet he corrected their shortcomings without rancor. When the disciples express their desire for worldly greatness rather than humble serving, Jesus sets them straight without scolding (9:46 – 48). When they persist in their self-seeking, even when Jesus himself is under tremendous pressure, he corrects them mildly and adds an encouragement (22:24 – 30). Jesus comes across as a patient, merciful teacher of the way of mercy.

Many of us, I suspect, feel burdened by Jesus' call to perfection. We know that we fall far short of what he asks, and we feel bad about it. It is hard for us to conceive that he can be very happy with us given our inadequate response to his call to discipleship. Feeling discouraged, we may sometimes be tempted either to give up our attempt to follow him or to adopt a lower set of expectations — to measure ourselves by a lesser standard, according to which we seem to be doing okay and deserve to feel that Jesus is pleased with us. This involves persuading ourselves that our sins are not so bad (or perhaps are not really sins at all), that our selfishness is not really a problem.

We would do better to accept Jesus as Luke portrays him, with both his high expectations and his limitless mercy. Judged according to his standard — "Be merciful, just as your Father is merciful" (6:36) — we can only admit that we are still far from being what he expects. But then, our failure does not diminish his love for us. Our falling short will not stop him from inviting himself to dinner in our home. He will continue to offer his friendship in heartfelt love, for he wills our good even more than we do.

The Only Limit to God's Mercy

Further Thoughts on the Rich Man and Lazarus, from a Sermon by St. John Chrysostom

Is there a limit to God's mercy? Jesus' parable of the rich man and Lazarus (Luke 16:19 – 31) suggests the answer is both no and yes. Fundamentally no, for God is merciful, simply and absolutely. But yes, inasmuch as our own lack of mercy can cut us off from God's mercy. The only limit to God's mercy toward us is the limit we set up.

Around the year 390 St. John Chrysostom, a priest at the cathedral in Antioch in present-day Turkey urged his large, urban congregation to reflect on this message in Jesus' parable. To feel the full effect of John's portrayal of the wealthy man's fate, it is helpful to realize that wealthy people in the ancient world were constantly surrounded by servants, even when they slept. The idea of being left completely alone would have been especially disturbing to John's wealthy parishioners.

Here are excerpts from his sermon:

While we are here, we have a useful hope. But when we go to that place, we no longer have it in our power to repent and be cleansed of our sins. So we must constantly prepare for leaving this world. What if it should please the Lord to call us this evening or tomorrow? The future is uncertain, so we should be constantly engaged in the struggle and ready to make a dignified departure — just as Lazarus was continually patient and persevering, which is why he was escorted off with such great honor.

The rich man also died and was buried. Beloved, do not skip over the statement "He was buried." The silver-ornamented tables, the couches, the carpets, the tapestries, and all the other furniture, the perfumes, the spices, the stores of wine, the different cuts of meat, the sauces, the cooks, the flatterers, the guards, the servants, and the rest of the parade — all are extinguished and have died away. Everything is ashes; everything is ashes and dust, lamentations and wailing, for no one can help anymore. No one can bring back the departed soul.

Now the power of gold and material abundance is put to the test. From such a great body of attendants he was led off naked and alone, from such great plenty he was unable to carry anything; but solitary, without a guide, he was taken away. None of those who had cared for him, none of those who had assisted him, was there to deliver him from the punishment. Dragged away from all of these, he receives his deserved punishment, bearing the unbearable retribution alone.

In light of the reversal that Lazarus and the rich man experienced after death, John spurred his listeners to consider the deceptive nature of earthly wealth:

Now the rich man is the one seeking help from the poor man, begging from the table of this man who used to lie hungry, exposed to the dogs' mouths. The situation is reversed! Now everyone learns who was the rich man and who was the poor man — learns that Lazarus was the most richly supplied of all, while the other was the poorest of all.

For as actors step out onto the stage wearing the masks of kings and generals and physicians and public speakers and professors and soldiers, even though they themselves are nothing of the sort, just so in the present life, poverty and wealth are only masks. If you are sitting in the theater and see one of the players down on the stage with the mask of a king, you do not think that he really is a king or wish to become like him, because you know that he is an ordinary man on the street, a water carrier, perhaps, or a metalworker, or something of that kind. Looking at his mask and his costume, you do not think he is fortunate or make any judgment about his social status.

In the very same way, sitting here in the world, as though in a theater, and watching the players on the stage, when you see many wealthy people, do not think that they are really wealthy, but rather that they are wearing the masks of wealthy people. For just as that one who is playing the king or the general on the stage often happens to be a servant or one of the hawkers of figs and grapes in the market, so also this wealthy man often happens to be the poorest of all. If you were to remove his mask and open his conscience and enter his mind, you would find a great poverty of goodness and discover that he is the least honorable of people.

In theaters, when evening comes on and those who have been sitting together depart, those who had appeared to everyone as kings and generals go outside and put off their impressive theatrical costumes and are seen now as they really are. In the same way, when death arrives and the theater is dissolved, everyone, putting off the masks of wealth and poverty, goes there, and being evaluated on their actions alone, some are seen to be truly wealthy, others poor, some worthy of honor, some to be held in no esteem.

Often, at all events, one of those who are wealthy here is found there to be the poorest of all, as indeed the rich man in the parable. For when evening came, that is to say, death, and he went out from the theater of the present life, and he put off his mask, he appeared as the poorest of all, so poor as not to own a drop of water but to have to beg for it — and not get what he begged for. What poverty could be poorer than this?

But what exactly was the rich man's sin? It is implied rather than stated explicitly in the parable: a failure to show mercy. John's sermon draws out the principle involved and applies it to the more affluent members of the congregation:

This also is theft: not to share one's possessions. For not only stealing others' possessions but also refusing to share with others one's own possessions is theft. It is taking too large a share; it is withholding what belongs to others.

Money belongs to the Lord, no matter how we acquired it. And if we supply it to those who stand in need of it, we will make a great abundance for ourselves. Indeed, this is why God allowed you to have more — not to waste it on prostitution and drunkenness and gluttony and extravagant expenditures on clothing and other forms of indolence, but to divide it up among the needy.

If an official in the royal treasury is entrusted with funds but neglects to disburse them as he is instructed and instead lavishes them on his own indolence, he suffers punishment and is put to death. In the same way the wealthy person is a recipient of money that ought to be distributed to the poor. He is commanded to distribute it to the needy among his fellow servants. If, then, he spends more on himself than what he needs by nature, he will suffer the harshest punishment. For his possessions do not belong to him, but to his fellow servants!

Let us use our possessions sparingly, then, as the property of others, so that our possessions may become truly ours. But how shall we use our possessions sparingly, as the property of others? When we do not spend them beyond our needs or on ourselves alone, but share them out among the needy.

If you are well off and spend more on yourself than you need, you will give an account of the possessions entrusted to you. In fact, this happens in great households. For many people entrust their household funds to their stewards. But those who are entrusted with the funds, whatever they might prefer to do, keep watch over what has been given them. They do not avail themselves of what has been entrusted to them but instead distribute it according to the master's instructions.

You also, *do* this! For in fact you received more than others — you were entrusted with more — not so that you would spend it only on yourself but so that you would also become a good steward on behalf of others.

Suggestions for Bible Discussion Groups

Like a camping trip, a Bible discussion group works best if you agree on what you're undertaking together, why you're doing it, where you hope to get to, and how you intend to get there. Many groups use their first meeting to reach a consensus on such questions. Here is a checklist of issues, with a few bits of advice from people with experience in Bible discussions. (A planning discussion will go more smoothly if the leaders have thought through the following issues beforehand.)

Agree on your purpose. Are you getting together to gain wisdom and direction for your life? to finally get acquainted with the Bible? to support one another in following Christ? to encourage those who are exploring — or reexploring — the Church? for other reasons?

Agree on attitudes. For example: "We're all beginners here." "We're here to help each other understand and respond to God's Word." "We're not here to offer counseling or direction to each other." "We want to read Scripture prayerfully." What do *you* wish to emphasize? Make it explicit!

Agree on ground rules. Barbara J. Fleischer, in her useful book *Facilitating for Growth,* recommends that a group clearly state its approach to the following:

✦ Preparation. Do we agree to read the material before each meeting?

✦ Attendance. What kind of priority will we give to our meetings?

✦ Self-revelation. Are we willing to help the others in the group gradually get to know us — our weaknesses as well as our strengths, our needs as well as our gifts?

✦ Listening. Will we commit ourselves to listening to each other?

✦ Confidentiality. Will we keep everything that is shared with the group in the group?

✦ Encouragement and support. Will we give as well as receive?

+ Participation. Will we work to allow everyone time and opportunity to make a contribution?

You could probably take a pen and draw a circle around
listening and *confidentiality*. Those two points are especially
important.

The following items could be added to Fleischer's list:

+ Relationship with parish. Is our group part of the religious education program? independent, but operating with the express
approval of the pastor? not a parish-based group at all?

+ New members. In the course of the six meetings, will new
members be allowed?

Agree on housekeeping.

+ When will we meet?

+ How often will we meet? Meeting weekly or every other week
is best if you can manage it. William Riley remarks, "Meetings
once a month are too distant from each other for the threads
of the last session not to be lost" *(The Bible Study Group: An
Owner's Manual).*

+ How long will meetings run?

+ Where will we meet?

+ Is any setup needed? Christine Dodd writes that "the problem
with meeting in a place like a church hall is that it can be very
soul-destroying" given the cold, impersonal feel of many church
facilities. If you have to meet in a church facility, Dodd recommends doing something to make the area homey *(Making Scripture Work).*

+ Who will host the meetings? Leaders and hosts are not necessarily identical.

+ Will we have refreshments? Who will provide them?

✦ What about child care? Most experienced leaders of Bible discussion groups discourage bringing infants or other children to adult Bible discussions.

Agree on leadership. You need someone to facilitate — to keep the discussion on track, to see that everyone has a chance to speak, to help the group stay on schedule. Rena Duff, editor of the newsletter *Sharing God's Word Today,* recommends having two or three people take turns leading the discussions.

It's okay if the leader is not an expert regarding the Bible. You have this booklet, and if questions come up that no one can answer, you can delegate a participant to do a little research between meetings. It's important for the leader to set an example of listening, to draw out the quieter members (and occasionally restrain the more vocal ones), to move the group on when they get stuck, to remind the members of their agreements, and to summarize what the group is accomplishing.

Bible discussion is an opportunity to experience the fulfillment of Jesus' promise "Where two or three are gathered in my name, I am there among them" (Matthew 18:20). Put your discussion group in Jesus' hands. Pray for the guidance of the Spirit. And have a great time exploring God's Word together!

Suggestions for Individuals

Y ou can use this booklet just as well for individual study as for group discussion. While discussing the Bible with other people can be a rich experience, there are advantages to individual reading. For example:

✦ You can focus on the points that interest you most.

✦ You can go at your own pace.

✦ You can be completely relaxed and unashamedly honest in your answers to all the questions, since you don't have to share them with anyone else!

My suggestions for using this booklet on your own are these:

✦ Don't skip "Questions to Begin." The questions can help you as an individual reader warm up to the topic of the reading.

✦ Take your time on "Questions for Careful Reading" and "Questions for Application." While a group will probably not have enough time to work on all the questions, you can allow yourself the time to consider all of them if you are using the booklet by yourself.

✦ If you are going through Luke at your own pace, consider reading the entire Gospel, not just the parts excerpted in this booklet. "Between Discussions" pages will give you some guidance in reading the additional portions of Luke. Your total understanding of the Gospel will be greatly increased by reading through Luke from beginning to end.

✦ Since you control the pace, give yourself plenty of opportunities to reflect on the meaning of the Gospel for you. Let your reading be an opportunity for Luke's words to become God's words to you.

The following editions of the Bible contain the full set of biblical books recognized by the Catholic Church, along with a great deal of useful explanatory material:

+ The Catholic Study Bible (Oxford University Press), which uses the text of the New American Bible

+ The Catholic Bible: Personal Study Edition (Oxford University Press), which also uses the text of the New American Bible

+ The New Jerusalem Bible, the regular (not the reader's) edition (Doubleday)